AFRICA
TO
AMERICA
A JOURNEY OF FAITH

DIANE GERBER

Africa to America: A Journey of Faith

Trilogy Christian Publishers
A Wholly Owned Subsidiary of Trinity Broadcasting Network
2442 Michelle Drive, Tustin, CA 92780

Manufactured in the United States of America

Trilogy Disclaimer: The views and content expressed in this book are those of the author and may not nec-essarily reflect the views and doctrine of Trilogy Christian Publishing or the Trinity Broadcasting Network.

10 9 8 7 6 5 4 3 2 1
Library of Congress Cataloging-in-Publication Data is available.

ISBN: 978-1-63769-600-2
E-ISBN: 978-1-63769-601-9

DEDICATION

This book is dedicated to my husband and two children.
With love.

As I come to the place
of the Red, White and Blue
I have been to the land
where the green grass is true
I was born in the bush
Where you can hear the lions roar
I am saying to you
This is my life story
And I am sharing it with you

PART ONE

THE REPUBLIC OF SOUTH AFRICA

I had moved back to the small town of Tzaneen due to the death of my mother. I was originally from Johannesburg, and I had moved to Tzaneen when my father was transferred for work. My dad's family was originally from Cornwall and had moved to South Africa to work on the gold mines in Johannesburg. Even though he was born in South Africa, he still made the best pasties on this side of the Tamar River. I had traveled and lived in Cape Town for a few years but now found myself back in Tzaneen. Tzaneen is a small farm town situated in the Limpopo province in the Valley of the Elephants. It is 45 minutes from the Kruger National Park (referred to by the locals as just Kruger), two hours south of Zimbabwe, and two hours west of Mozambique.

It is a lush sub-tropical town, with a huge farming community, orchards of bananas, avocados, lychees and tea plantations on the hillside as far as the eye can see. It is surrounded by the Wolkberg mountains and is sustained by the picturesque Tzaneen Dam. The Letaba River feeds the dam and then flows all the way through the Kruger National Park where it converges with the Olifants River, the Limpopo River at the foothills of the Limbombo Mountains (the border between South Africa and Mozambique), and finally into the Indian Ocean.

The river is the lifeblood of the Tzaneen community and far beyond as it is the main water supply for most of the farmers all the way to the Kruger National Park. It also provides water for household supply, drinking water for livestock, as well as a source of water for washing as I would often see the local African ladies doing their laundry in the water and drying the clothes on the rocks.

The African community is made up of the Tsonga and Northern Sotho tribes. The white community is made up mainly of Afrikaner people (those from Dutch descent) with a small minority of English, Portuguese, and other nationalities.

Originally, being from the city of Johannesburg (four and a half hours south of Tzaneen), I found life in this small town fascinating. I was used to the bright lights and the up-all-night atmosphere of Johannesburg, buzzing with nightlife and entertainment. With a downtown full of things to do. I loved movies, the theatre, and eating out. I really enjoyed watching sports, but I was not very competitive and never actually played any sort of sport. I preferred to cheer from the sidelines. There were three things I was absolutely passionate about: reading, flowers and animals. My younger brother Graham was away at boarding school during the year and when I was alone, I used to love shopping. When I say I love shopping … well, I only love shopping for books. I would and still often get lost in the pages of a good book!

My favorites being about mystery, time-travel, or history, and on Saturday mornings I would enjoy a walk around looking for the perfect escape in the pages of a new book. I loved sitting in the morning sun at my favorite coffee shop enjoying my latest adventure.

Tzaneen was a little different and Saturday mornings were all about the farmers markets and church fetes. I'll never forget going to a morning market and watching how the Afrikaans ladies made and sold pancakes in the parking lot. This was something I had to get used to. Due to the fact that my schooling in Johannesburg and Kwazulu-Natal had been in English, my Afrikaans was very limited, so I had to learn very quickly as I muddled through my first parking lot pancake purchase.

The English community was very tight knit, part of which was made up of some very prominent farming families who had a lot of land and a lot of money, most of them had been in Tzaneen for generations and, initially, I felt very much like an outsider.

I was very blessed to have Jean, a dear friend whom I had met a few years before when I was living in Kwazulu-Natal. Even though she lived in another part of the country, I knew she was only a phone-call away. At this time of change in my life, she was wonderfully supportive and always had positive advice. Being quite a bit older than me, I always referred to her as "Aunty Jean".

After about two years of arriving in Tzaneen, I had found my niche. I was working in a clothing store on the high street (or the only street), and I had become friends with some of the Portuguese immigrants that had arrived from Mozambique and Angola. My dad had remarried and now my brother and I had five new Afrikaans step siblings, four sisters and a brother.

One chilly winter's Saturday, a friend of my brother's needed a ride to soccer practice. I offered him a lift, and he asked if we could pick up another friend of his. This friend's name was Terence, and I was totally unaware how offering one person a lift could change the fate of my whole life.

Terence was the complete opposite to me in so many ways. He was born and raised in Tzaneen, and his family were very prominent, you could not go anywhere without everyone knowing who you were. He had two older sisters Ruth and Jeanette, who were twins and a younger brother, Brian. He was a very good sportsman and very competitive! Growing up on a farm in this part of the country he was an avid outdoorsman. He loved nature and camping, and wherever he and his family went their fishing rods were right there with them. The Kruger National Park was like a second home to him. He had gone there since he was a baby. On paper, it would never had worked, but we were drawn to each other. We both loved sport and animals, but there was one more thing that we had in common. Terence had just come home from spending two years traveling abroad. He had worked on a kibbutz in Israel, and then had spent time traveling through Europe with a friend. He had only been back a short while before we met, and even though he was a local he somehow thought differently.

Being away from a small town can do that. He and I were both liberal in our views of apartheid, and we did not agree with it. It was almost radical thinking in the 70's compared to how most people were in those days.

We spent the next year dating, and my favorite Saturday night dates would be when we would go to the local cinema which Terence's uncle and aunt owned. When he and his siblings were little kids, they used to usher at Gerber's Cinema getting to see the latest movies free as payment. The little cinema was famous in Tzaneen and had stood the test of time in this town by keeping current and only showing the latest movies. It was definitely not what I was used to, but it was quaint, and I loved it! The doors were purple, and the inside smelled of popcorn and cigarette smoke — not ideal, but it had such a feeling of nostalgia. Terence's mom was a very independent woman, and I have more than one memory of her wielding a gun and shooting the dangerous snakes that had ventured too close to the house. However, she was unable to drive and so on the nights that Terence's dad worked late she ended up being stuck on the farm. Those nights she would join us for movies! It was so funny, and I can't help but smile when I think back. She would sit right down in between us without even thinking. The only way we got to speak to each other was to talk over her!

During intervals our friends would tease Terence asking why a 29 year old man needed a chaperon. But his mom was chatting up a storm with all the other locals catching up on local gossip and what was happening in and around Tzaneen. Once the interval was over, there she was again right back in the middle of us none the wiser, and the two of us would just smile.

Another place Terence introduced me to was the Kruger National Park. It is an amazing place. Once you entered the park it was as if you had entered another world. It was so peaceful, bushveld as far as the eye could see. We would drive along the tar or dirt roads for hours looking to see the most amazing African animals including the Big Five (Lion, Leopard, Elephant, Buffalo, and Rhinoceros) as well as so many other mammals and birds. He knew how much I love animals, and soon enough the Park became a place I loved as much as Terence did. We would get up early some Sundays and pack a small picnic of snacks and drinks in a cooler for the car. We would enter the park at the Phalaborwa gate and slowly make our way to the Letaba camp, which was the closest camp to the gate, where we would always have lunch in the beautiful restaurant which overlooked the Letaba river, which had made its way here all the way from the Tzaneen dam. You could just tell by looking at it that the river was at home here, meandering through the tall fig trees that embraced its banks. There would be so much life around the river, and as we sat on the veranda eating our lunch, we would watch the elephants drinking and playing in the water. They were always accompanied by giraffe, waterbuck, some warthogs and many other smaller antelope.

Every now and then, hippos would make a fuss by grunting as a crocodile came too close to the herd wallowing in the shallows.

The small vervet monkeys were always great entertainment as they would linger around the restaurants looking for treats from visitors only to be chased by a ranger or waiter!

After lunch, we would take a short walk along the fence of the camp which overlooked the river and sit on one of the benches placed there. In summer, the warm breeze would bring the smell of the bushveld, and I would close my eyes and breathe it in being mesmerized by the smell and sounds of what can only be found in Africa.

South Africa
It is time, it is time
The wild is calling, the sun is rising
The monkeys are looking, the birds are singing
South Africa, South Africa
The day has begun

After a year of dating Terence, he proposed, then after a year of being engaged we got married in the August of 1979. We had often thought of traveling and leaving South Africa. We ourselves did not want to live in a nation of suppression of our fellow man or in a nation of hatred, and we did not want our future family to grow up in that sort of environment either.

However, life happens — in a few short years Terence had become a partner in a supermarket franchise, with part ownership of one store in Tzaneen and one in Duiwelskloof, the neighboring town twenty minutes away.

We had two children Jade and Joffre, and we were living on Terence's family farm just outside of town. The farm had two beautiful homes, one for our family and one where Terence's parents lived. In between the 2 houses stood a majestic flamboyant tree. During the summer months it's flame red and orange flowers formed a beautiful canopy making sure the tree lived up to it's other name: the flame tree. One year when we came home from our beach holiday to find that Terence's dad had built an amazing double story tree house right in the middle of the tree as a welcome home surprise for the children. I think Terence was the one that was most surprised as after a long drive home of about 12 hours, he found his first night home was not in his own bed but in the treehouse! Joffre loved the treehouse, and he and his friends spent many days up there in a world of their own. We had a huge garden, swimming pool and entertaining area. Our farm extended down to the Letaba River where we owned the riverbank and part of the river which was important for water rights. The riverbank was lush and full of trees, and we spend many afternoons walking along the banks, fishing and swimming. One of my favorite memories of the river was one Palm Sunday. We decided to skip church that morning — well church in the regular sense. We woke up early at sunrise and took our children to the river. There was a huge rock that formed part of a small waterfall where we set up our church service for the morning. We found some reeds along the riverbank and broke them off to make small crosses. Each of us made our cross and then sat on the blanket we brought with while Terence read the story of Palm Sunday.

After our service in nature and watching the sunrise, we said a prayer for the beginning of Holy Week, we then tossed the crosses we made into the water and watched them float away. It was beautiful. I sat alone on the rock while Terence went with the children as they followed the crosses downstream. I watched them, and my heart was overflowing with joy.

The farm had avocado, nartjie, mango and lychee orchards. Even though they produced fruit, we never actually farmed them; we used them for household use. Our lives were idyllic, but all that was about to change.

Our family movie night abruptly came to an end when we heard a group of men shouting and running through our back garden. They had breached the fence on our property and seemed to be chasing someone. Terence quickly turned off all the lights and told me and the children to go and hide, making sure we were away from any windows. He opened the kitchen door and spoke to the men through the bars of the security gate that we had recently installed and asked the men what was going on. They told him that the man they were chasing had just murdered someone during a late-night card game, and they were hunting him down to kill him. After assuring them we had not seen this man and we were not harboring him, they left and continued their search on the next farm.

Over the past few years, we had often discussed the possibility of immigrating. We would read up on places we could go to, what skills were required, how the schooling systems worked, the cost of housing as well as the requirements of working visas and eventually citizenship. We even considered going to live on a Kibbutz in Israel.

Now however, violence was starting to creep into our everyday lives and tonight was the first taste of that. Later that night while we were lying in bed, Terence turned to me and said that he thinks we need to seriously make plans to leave the country.

1991

During the early 70's, one of Terence's older sisters, Ruth, had taken a trip to the USA with her husband Douglas and baby son Ernest of eighteen months. They had decided to stay in the USA and start their new lives across the Atlantic.

After becoming an American citizen, Ruth had been coming out to South Africa on holiday and telling the family how wonderful life was there. Terence had asked her if there was any way that he and his family could immigrate. In 1991, she had brought with her the immigration forms for us to complete. She would stand as a sponsor for her brother and his family — namely, me and our two children. Jade was eleven and Joffre was eight.

We filled out the forms and were told the process would take about seven years, and so the wait began.

All we could do was continue to live our lives until we heard from the US Immigration. Terence was a business owner, Lion's club treasurer, and church deacon. I was a homemaker helping and supporting my family whenever and wherever I could. I volunteered at the after-school lunch program, and two days a week I would do the books for Terence's business, and on Friday mornings I would work together with the church landscaper, Joseph gardening and landscaping the church ground, gardens and flower beds.

Both my children had the privilege of growing up on a farm in Africa experiencing the delights of nature from the vervet monkeys stealing fruit from the trees in the garden to the lonely hippopotamus that would forage in the cool of the evening (remaining on the other side of the fence) much to the frustration of the dogs.

Jade and Joffre attended the local primary school called Unicorn Primary School. It was a small co-ed school where everyone knew everyone, a wonderful safe haven which was an amazing foundation for each child's future.

1992

The auctioneer's hammer hit the wood. Sold!

It was all gone. Our cars. Our home. Our farm. Our lives. But not our faith.

Our business endeavor had not worked. After 12 years of supermarket retail, Terence went into a bakery business supplying small businesses in the rural areas with bread. This was a political and violent time in South Africa. A three-month boycott of all businesses owned by white people in the area, combined with other factors, caused the company to fold. The week of our grand opening, the boycott started. Besides the fact that the local businesses owned by black people would not be purchasing any of our products, there had also been threats on the employees' lives. The delivery drivers' lives were in danger. Word had spread via the "bush telegraph" that any deliveries made on behalf of white business owners would be hijacked. The load would be stolen and destroyed, and the driver would be murdered. Under no circumstance would Terence allow this to happen to any of his employees and so all deliveries would put on hold until further notice. As the stock was perishable, most of it had to be thrown away before it started to rot. One of the organizers of the boycott approached Terence with an offer. He said that none of the drivers would be harmed, and his products would be bought. This decision came at a heavy price. A large sum of money would go to the worker's unions in exchange for business. Blackmail. But blackmail comes with no guarantees and so Terence stood his ground and said no! He would not risk lives, his reputation or his beliefs to make money.

The factory was put on hold.

After the three-month boycott was over, we were hanging on by a thread. We saw the silver lining, and we were all excited when the factory reopened and production started once again. A few days later one of the employees noticed mold growing on and in all the bags of yeast. He called Terence right away and after a thorough inspection he came to the inevitable conclusion that all the yeast was unusable had to be thrown away. This was just too great a loss for us, and we were not able to recover financially. Terence had to file for bankruptcy.

We had literally lost everything…

I will never forget the day that he told me we had lost everything. My legs collapsed under me as I fell on the couch, not able to breathe, not able to cry, not able to think. I had no idea what to do. I felt so helpless there seemed like no way out. Terence was just as devastated as I was. He soon left the house to meet up with the lawyers in town.

My heart ached for him.

I got up and moved towards the window — our lives were over. Emotionless and numb I stood there, staring into nothing. Where do we go from here? We had two children; what would happen to them? Terence's parents lived on the property. Where would they go? Graham and his fiancé had started to build a home on the bank of our river front — what would happen to them? What would happen to our animals? Our family had one rule with animals — if we can't keep them, we euthanize them. We would never give our animals away. How were we going to deal with all this? All these thoughts just kept playing over and over in my mind as I stood there for what seemed to be an eternity. My mind was in turmoil,

I wanted to pray out loud, but my mouth would not move to say the words.

All of a sudden, a strange peace came over me. Warmth covered me like someone had put their arms around me, and I knew right then that it was my Heavenly Father holding me as His child and reassuring me all of this was going to work out. But I would still have a long way to go.

We owed a lot of debt, and our family, especially Terence became the topic of a lot of stares, the stories, the gossip we encountered. Sadly, it was spread by strangers, friends and family alike. Some true, most untrue. Terence's parents were wonderful and more than understanding. Terence's younger brother Brian and his oldest daughter May-Lin lived in Witbank, a mining city three hours away. His mom and dad would have to move to Witbank and leave the town and the lives they had lived for almost 60 years. Sadly, Graham and his fiancé also lost their home on our land. This had such a ripple effect and had impacted the lives of so many more people than just Terence and me. The dawning of each day brought new challenges, mainly emotional. Who was I going to meet in the street? At the school? In the supermarket, the one he previously part owned? And what they had heard about us? True or untrue, it did not matter. Some friends would offer condolences and help at every turn while others would just completely ignore me as if we had never met. The one thing I feared most was that Terence would have to go to jail. I think I made the lawyer want to pull her hair out because I kept asking her, and she kept reassuring me that he would not go to jail.

He had not done anything illegal. I just feared the worst with regards to the debtors and thought that if we could not pay, they would arrest him.

A few times during the turmoil, I would think of our immigration and wondering how our paperwork was progressing.

How I wish we could just escape. Just leave everything behind. Start anew, start afresh. However, it was just a dream, with our huge financial loss we had to put the USA to the back of our minds, at this point it was not even a dream, it was an impossibility.

1993

This year was the most difficult for us financially. We had absolutely minimal income. Even though the factory was bankrupt, we had been given a second chance to pay our debts and keep our home. Terence had been offered a temporary position at the supermarket he had once co-owned, and he had gone back to the work for his old partners at the Duiwelskloof location. I was looking for a job and even though I had been the bookkeeper for Terence there was nothing available in Tzaneen. Even though Graham and his fiancé has taken a huge financial loss with the loss of our farm — he had generously lent us some money to buy some second-hand jackets in all shapes and sizes. For about two months, Terence, Graham and I would drive into town and sell the jackets from the trunk of his car. I felt we stood out like sore thumbs, but honestly, it was only my pride. Nobody seemed to think anything of it, and if they did, we never heard about it. Sadly, it was not very successful, and we sold most of them under cost just to get rid of them. Not only did we now owe him for the loss of his home, we owed him more for the jackets. No matter what we did — it just was not enough.

While all the legal stuff was being sorted out and we were still in talks of how to save the factory, we were still able to stay on the farm. Winter was approaching, and on the weekends, Terence would work the land preparing it for winter vegetables. That winter we harvested cabbage, carrots, onions and fennel. There was also a small harvest of lemons and nartjies from the trees planted by Terence's father about 20 years ago. Up until now they had been for household use, but now they were saving our lives. I would gather a selection of citrus fruit and the winter vegetables and pack them into shallow cardboard boxes and drive into town on a Friday morning to the local market. I would sell about 10 boxes on a Friday, and then I had between ten and fifteen regular customers, friends and strangers alike that I would personally deliver to. I would make the boxes as attractive as possible and would include a bible verse in the box to encourage and uplift those who bought them. No matter what was happening in my life, I wanted to make sure that I was still encouraging others and keeping my faith alive and strong, even though most of the time I felt like I was the one that needed to receive the encouragement. Some Fridays it would take all my physical strength to get out of bed and put the boxes together. It would take even more strength to take the drive into town and sell my wares. I would always feel better and smile when I saw my customer read the bible verse. You never know what others are going through and maybe — through me — they received a word they needed. The winter boxes were a success but as all things, they came to an end with the approach of summer.

That year for my birthday a friend of mine gave me a copy of Catherine Marshall's book, *The Comforter*. What a blessing that little book was to become over the next few days, months, and years. I mentioned to my friend what a wonderful gift the book had been. The following Christmas she blessed me with another one of Catherine Marshall's books, *The Helper*. I poured over each page which is now covered in pencil notes and dates that I wrote during my daily quiet time and in moments of feeling complete helplessness. Reading through the books now, I can see how God was right in the midst of the problems even though I had days when I felt He had abandoned my family and I.

He was always there.

Summers in Tzaneen were hot and humid, and this one was no different except for the fact that we had the extra burden of our finances. During this time, I remember on numerous occasions driving home after picking up the children from school and us putting all our coins together to see if we had enough money for a loaf of bread. We seemed to live on bread and potatoes for a lot of our meals and some of the poorer quality vegetables we had not sold. Luckily, we were still on the farm. We had had a season of good winter rains and the old lychee trees had started to bear fruit. The trees were bursting at the seams with red, delicious fruit! It was like a gift from God reminding us that He would provide. I decided to buy some lychee boxes at the local co-op on account and start picking the fruit to sell.

Each day after school and homework, we would have a small lunch and then we would all go out into the orchards and hand pick lychees. My only concern besides the heat was snakes. Over the years, we had seen our fair share of Rinkhals snakes also known as the ring-necked spitting cobras and black mambas on the farm. Even though it was hot, we would all have to wear thick socks, closed shoes and long pants as a small protection for a snakebite but better than nothing. We all knew that if anyone of us got bitten by the black mamba we would have about twenty minutes to get the doctor in town before any permanent damage took effect.

It was hard going for the children and I. I did most of the heavy lifting, Jade was 13 and now in her final year of primary school, and Joffre was only 10, but they did their best to help out. No matter what we were going through at home, they both still did well at school in the classroom and on the sports field. Once we had picked them, we had to weigh and pack them, then Terence would take them into town the next morning and sell them at the supermarket. I thought to myself what a long cry off from the city girl I had been 15 years prior.

1994

At this point in time there were two things that we needed. Firstly, Terence needed a permanent job. We needed to make ends meet for our family as well as pay off the debts from the factory, and secondly, we needed a place to live. I am not sure what was worse — not having money for food or driving down the main street with huge posters everywhere saying, "Gerber Farm - liquidation auction."? It was heartbreaking — our family had been reduced to a poster in the main street, our lives on full display for everyone. Even though the events had been not of our own doing we still felt responsible, and it took all the courage we had to walk down the street with our heads held high.

With his experience and reputation in the retail world, Terence received job offers from all over the country. How easy it would have been to just move away from everything, leave it all behind. There was a very good job prospect in Johannesburg. Terence and I discussed the situation; we then spoke to our children about it. Jade had just started high school at Merensky High School which was between Tzaneen and Duiwelskloof set amongst lush vegetation with views of the distant mountains which made it one of the most picturesque schools in the country. Joffre went on to attend Kings Court Christian School perched amongst the blue gum trees on the hill overlooking the town of Duiwelskloof. We would not want to uproot them. They were also farm children and could not bear the thought of moving to a big city where they would know no one. We were, however, desperate and did not want to pass up a good opportunity. So, we took the trip up to Johannesburg, and Terence met with the supermarket owner. We looked at the area and possible housing prospects but, in the end, we decided to stay in Tzaneen. Terence decided to accept a job offer at a locally owned mini market in Duiwelskloof. Being only twenty minutes away from Tzaneen lots of locals either worked in Tzaneen and lived in Duiwelskloof or the other way around, so this was not anything out of the ordinary. Also due to the fact that Joffre's school was there seemed to be perfect. The only difference was that this shop was literally a stone's throw away from the previous supermarket Terence had once co-owned. The owner of this mini market had been an acquaintance of Terence's for years and was more than happy to have him as his store manager.

One day about two weeks before Terence started his new job, Aunty Jean called me and told me that she had booked a holiday for the five of us. She wanted to treat us and give us a chance to "get away from it all". She had rented a small apartment on the South Coast of Kwazulu-Natal, just a stone's throw away from the beach and the warm waves of the Indian Ocean. We had a fantastic week! It was good to spend time with Aunty Jean again.

Rumors were spreading about where Terence was working, and I remember one Saturday evening after supper, Terence telling me that some of the local men we knew from Tzaneen had heard about his new job. There was a cricket practice ground about a mile from the shop, and they had all stopped in to buy refreshments after practice and to confirm that the rumors about Terence were true. After that incident, word spread like wildfire; needless to say, we were learning to handle the gossip by God's grace. At this point I had to start looking for a job. I had always been a stay-at-home mom, but now I had to start looking for work to help with the basics around the house and for our children. I was offered a morning only job at a local service station that was owned by an elderly couple in our church. This was a real blessing as I was able to spend the afternoons with the children when they got out of school.

With Terence and I both now working, we needed a place to live. A family friend had a house built on their farm for one of their sons. The son, however, had decided to move back to Australia just weeks before we lost our home and farm, and so very kindly, the house was offered to us. We ended up renting that house for the next ten years.

What a blessing — God was providing everything that we needed, above and beyond as only He can. On the day our property and personal items were to be auctioned, Terence's boss accompanied Terence, offering to buy back any items that we needed. Terence was astonished, but the only thing we really needed was a car, and so he bought our car back from the bank for us. (We had received an anonymous gift of money which allowed us to buy back some of our furniture from the bank.) The finality of losing the farm was short lived as we had a week to move and leave our home.

On the last day of the move, some members of our church family helped us with the heavy furniture. By that evening we were exhausted, thank goodness we had a delicious meal cooked for us. The next day was Sunday after church, Terence went off to work, and the children, our pets and I went exploring our new environment. It was a beautiful house — plain but beautiful. It was a renovated farm shed, so it was quite spacious. The house had five bedrooms, three bathrooms, an open plan lounge and dining room with a huge kitchen, laundry and a long veranda on the one side.

The house was built on a slight incline overlooking an acre of lawn. It was fenced in with diamond fencing on which climbed the most beautiful, bright colored Bougainvillea. It was like a small haven surrounded by colors of bright red, orange, and cerise. Beyond the fence was the Tzaneen dam. The Wolkberg mountain range was in the distance and seemed to be the perfect backdrop. It was the most beautiful sight, and to this day the sunsets we watched from the veranda are something I will never forget.

The African sunset, like none other
Over the waters, like a glowing orange rainbow
For the moon has come, and the sun has gone

The house was built between a mango farm owned by one farmer and an avocado farm owned by our friend and new landlord. There were many summer evenings when we would have a chat with either farmer who was walking through his orchards. We were given one of the avocado trees for our own use. And after a few months of living there the mango farmer gave us a mango tree of our very own too! Amazingly, our dogs enjoyed the avocados more than the children did and would always eat the ones that fell from the trees. On our evening walks to the dam during the winter months, they would choose an avocado and hide it in the small indigenous bushes along the fence of the property picking it up on the way back and then lie on the lush front lawn enjoying it at their leisure.

The years had gone by without incident, but it was 1994 and the first ever general election was scheduled. We were all on high alert. The children's schools had even shut down for the week of the election in anticipation for political unrest. The election went smoothly, and South Africa's first black president Nelson Mandela was in power. There was no one better suited to be our president. Such a forgiving man. Such a proud man and such a visionary. I am proud to have lived in a South Africa where he was my president.

Unfortunately, we started to notice subtle problems, especially on the farms in that area of the Northern Province. The issues in Zimbabwe with land reforms were filtering through the borders and so we were getting a bit concerned. Every day was another farm attack, another rape, another friend that had been held up in their own house at gun point. Another murder that Terence's cousin (a local detective) had to be called out to. We had a security company take us on as one of their clients. We had two panic buttons which (when pressed) meant the security officers would hopefully come to our rescue before the attackers did us or our property any harm. If I was working out in the garden, I would wear the button around my neck. As well as the children, Miriam (our maid) was taught to keep all the doors locked if she was inside, and the only door open while she worked in the kitchen was the door leading into the car port which had large security gates that remained locked at all times. If Miriam was alone, she always had a panic button with her. Our dogs spent a lot of time in the car port or on the front veranda but slept inside every night. If there was going to be an attack it was normally in the early hours of the morning.

Everyone knew not to ever go outside to investigate. Neighbors were always willing to come to the rescue if they heard some kind of alarm or screaming.

1995 - 1996

In the summer months, (because of the high rainfall) it took a whole day to mow the lawn and nearly the whole week to trim the sixty plus bougainvillea around the property. Terence and I were struggling to keep up with the gardening. Once we were able to afford help, one of the farm workers recommended Sarah. He knew that she was looking for work and that we were looking for someone to help with the garden. Sarah was young, probably in her mid-20's but you could see that a hard life had taken its toll on her. She was slim but strong. She had sad eyes, but when she smiled it was the most infectious thing in the world. Sarah had a drinking problem and taking care of the garden became quite a challenge. When Sarah did not come to work it was often because she had too much to drink the night before or because she had been beaten by her boyfriend. We approached Sarah about reporting the beatings to the police — but she refused our help saying it would only make things worse.

On one particular Monday, Sarah arrived at work reeking of alcohol and complaining of back pains. Sarah and I usually spoke a mixture of English, Afrikaans, and Northern Sotho to each other and we got by but on this day, Sarah was too upset, and I could not understand what she was saying. With our housekeeper Miriam acting as an interpreter, we went into the kitchen and when she lifted her blouse and turned around; I discovered that she had two stab wounds in her back. I was horrified! How could someone have done this to Sarah? Unfortunately, this was not the worst of the injuries… she removed the scarf from her head to reveal another stab wound. This one in the back of her head! I felt sick! An overwhelming sense of sadness and anger came over me all at once, and I had to swallow the lump in my throat and push back the tears. It took me all my strength not to drive down to her house on the neighboring farm and give him a piece of my mind. I felt such empathy for this woman. The three of us just stood there for a minute. Silent. Miriam made her a very strong cup of tea which she loaded with sugar, made some toast and I gave her two pain pills. I knew that these would probably do nothing, and the physical pain was probably nothing compared to the horror she had experienced over the weekend. I checked my watch, and it was still half an hour till the local doctor's office opened. When Sarah had finished her tea and toast I drove her to the doctor. I waited with her and after the consultation I drove her home. I told her that she did not need to come to work until she was feeling better — not knowing how long that would be. She was insistent that I drop her off on the main tarred road. She said that she was feeling better and would walk down the small winding dirt road to her house. I watched with tears in my eyes as she walked away.

As I drove away, I prayed that she would be safe.

Even though Sarah told me in no uncertain terms not to call the police on her boyfriend, I did ask some of the other farm workers in the area who knew about her situation if there was anything I could do to help her in any way. Every one of them told me that if there was any outside interference, it would just make the situation worse for Sarah and her three little girls.

It had been almost five weeks since I had seen Sarah, I had asked around about her but no one was talking. I was sure she was dead. One day she was at work. Drawn and extremely thin, but she was back. I could only imagine what she had been through, and when I asked her again if she wanted to report it to the police, she got very defensive and said no. I felt that I should not press the issue. Her three little girls were delightful and in her own way she was a very good mother despite living under such sad circumstances. I was going to fire Sarah on many occasions due to her behavior, especially when she had been drinking but never had the heart to do it. In fact, we had many delightful days together over the ten years that she worked for us; she could be quite a comic. I fondly remember her cleaning the veranda with her third little girl firmly tied to her back as she was singing away, occasionally shouting at the dogs to move so she could sweep. Miriam kept the inside of our home as meticulous as Sarah kept the outside. Miriam had worked for my dad for many years, and when he moved Miriam came and worked for us. At the time, Joffre was a baby and Jade had just turned four. Miriam was a delight! And I only have the fondest memories of her. She was very short and rather round, and when she walked, she moved from side to side — similar to a penguin. She was so warm and gentle and always gave the best hugs. She would whistle while she worked and would always chuckle at the antics of my children or animals!

When we lost everything, unfortunately she lost her job. But we kept in touch and once we were able to pay her, she came back starting twice a week and eventually five days a week. Each morning I would drive the five kilometers to the local bus stop in town to pick her up, and in the afternoon took her back to catch her bus. My children and our dogs just adored her, and our Scotty would come with us every afternoon to drop Miriam off at the bus and would wail and wail when she left. She would say, "Goodbye Agnes," (his name was Angus) and much to her delight he would say goodbye to her in his own way and even stand on his two little short back legs and lean on the backseat watching her out the back window as we drove home, still crying until she was out of sight. Most of our animals only listened to her, so we all knew who the real head of the house was.

One morning during the school holidays, I had taken a few days off, and the children and I were busy in the house when we heard Miriam screaming from her bathroom on the lower level of the house. The first thing that came into my mind was that the farm was under attack. Any commotion was cause for real alarm. I yelled for the children to go into the one bedroom and lock the door. By this time the dogs were barking furiously. With my heart pounding, I unlocked the safe and had a gun ready in case I had to use it.

The next instant I saw Miriam running down the garden with her skirt round her waist. I chased after her screaming for her to stop and tell me what was going on. She pointed to the bathroom shouting "slang, slang" meaning "snake snake". I cautiously went into the bathroom found a huge black mamba had curled itself around the cistern of the toilet. The poor snake was looking for water and was probably more scared of all of us than we were of it. A real miracle that Miriam was not bitten. Sadly, we had to shoot the snake. It was one of our rules to only shoot snakes that were a danger to us or our animals. That afternoon Miriam was still shaking and muttering when I dropped her off at the bus. The indigenous people are very superstitious. To them, the only good snake is a dead snake. Miriam might have even visited the local witch doctor to find out why the snake was after her even though we knew better.

Every Friday Miriam would be wearing her brightest and best clothes; she would stand out at the crowded bus stop like a flower in full bloom, her round face beaming when I would tell her how beautiful she looked. Over the years we had our share of sad times (like when her husband died) and then happy times (like the birth of her new grandchild). Language was always a bit of a stumbling block but like with Sarah, Miriam and I had made our own language. During the corn season, Miriam would bring us corn from her small garden. She would cook them in salty water and would always smile when we came home, and she had surprised us with our favorite lunch! Even though she had very little, she was always willing to share and with such a good heart.

Over the years we spent at the farm we had some wonderful gatherings, mainly at Christmas. Being in the Southern hemisphere, Christmas was in the middle of summer. The flamboyant trees would spread their branches that were laden with bunches of their flame-like flowers, shading the lawn like huge umbrellas. During the evenings, there would be the heady scent of the frangipani flowers on the warm summer breeze, I would use the white and yellow blossoms to decorate the Christmas table which we had set out on the long veranda. Our family loves Christmas trees, and we would most definitely always have more than one. I recall one year we had five! We would usually decorate three of our trees in the garden and two in the lounge, a small one and a large one. At night, we would turn on the lights on the trees in the garden which Terence would always see in the distance as he returned home from work.

Most families would go away for Christmas visiting family and friends all over the country. Friends who did not go away for Christmas day would come over to our home. Our outside table would be laden with food contributed from each family and Christmas treats, especially the beloved Christmas crackers. We would have cooler boxes around the kitchen keeping the food cold; our fridge could not manage the load. We would play volleyball, cricket, and a special game of golf Joffre had invented. One year, our pastor anchored his boat on the shores of the dam at the bottom of the garden taking us all for a spin during the course of the day. Being hot and humid, afternoon tea and mince pies were followed by ice cold watermelon.

The 26th of December was Boxing Day for us. Most people spend the day at home. It is the day you eat the leftovers from the day before, relax and recover from Christmas day. Terence always worked on Boxing Day, so the children and I would normally go and visit our friends, James and Melissa, who lived on the local tea plantation.

1997

Jade had expressed her desire to travel and experience the world and its different cultures. In April of 1997, she set up a meeting with the current president of the Tzaneen Rotary Club. I remember as we sat in the car outside his office, and we held hands and prayed. We prayed that, if it be the right thing, God would guide her and open the doors. She wanted to represent Rotary as well as South Africa as a short-term Rotary Exchange Student. She was a straight A student, very involved in sport, as well as a variety of cultural events and nominated as Deputy Head Girl for her high school.

A week later we got a call from the president of our local Rotary club, the meeting was successful, and in December she would spend 6 weeks in a small town in Argentina. Not only would she experience this wonderful opportunity, but we would host her Rotary "sister" from her family in Argentina.

Our Spanish English dictionary was coming in very useful for Terence, Joffre and myself, and we had quite a few laughs at our pronunciation of most Spanish words.

The three of us took her on small day trips to all the attractions around Tzaneen and The Kruger National Park to show our part of the world.

Time was flying by, and we were heading into the last two weeks of our exchange program. We organized a ten-day trip to Zambia and Zimbabwe. We had the most amazing time visiting the beautiful city of Bulawayo where gracious old Jacaranda trees lined the wide streets. We also camped in the famous Hwange National Park which was an education for her as this was the first time she had ever slept in a tent. As fate would have it there was a horrendous thunderstorm that passed through Hwange on that same evening, and her first tenting experience was not the best. Early the next morning though, we were awoken by the guinea fowl and game in and around the camp. I think the leopard sighting was the most exciting and certainly made up for the previous night's bad weather.

Victoria Falls also known as "The Water that Thunders" was a highlight on our trip. When we arrived at the entrance to the falls, we were all handed a plastic yellow raincoat — at first, we were not sure why but after a few minutes we knew the reason. We spent one morning walking in the footsteps of early explorers our yellow raincoats glistening with water droplets from the spray of the falls as tons of water gushed over the rocks to the river flowing hundreds of feet below.

On the last leg of our trip we booked a canoe ride down the Zambezi River from Zambia to Zimbabwe. Our party of four was joined by some other guests from Holland and Australia as well as our four tour guides. As we glided down on the cool water, we kept our eyes open for game on the banks as well as in the water. A few sleek Impala antelope grazed the green grass on the riverbanks, and the ever-present vervet monkeys chatted and played in the majestic waterberry and fig trees that lined the river. Every now and again we would see small ears break the service of the water, those of the local hippo population. The tour guides were confident that the hippos were no threat just curious.

After spending the morning on the water, we stopped and ate lunch on the banks of the river. Our little party enjoyed sandwiches and cold drinks. After lunch we spent the rest of the afternoon heading downstream.

Once we had reached the end of our journey the guides pulled canoes out of the water, and we all sat chatting as we waited for the big truck to come and collect us and our equipment and take us back upstream to our vehicles. The afternoon was hot so Joffre and one of the other young men decided to take a last minute swim in the river with all four of the guides keeping watch as the crocodiles lurked nearby.

I remember watching Joffre in the water as the sun started to set on the horizon turning the water orange and pink. I sat there soaking up the African atmosphere thinking what a wonderful way to end our river safari.

Africa my Africa
Let's talk of the lion's roar
The king of the jungle
The one who controls all
The beast has spoken
He's made his claim
For all to see
Africa my Africa
The beast is king

At this same time, Jade was on the other side of the world in Argentina also going on trips with her host family to Uruguay and her fellow exchange students to Brazil and the famous Iguazu Falls.

1998

The new year seemed to be upon us, and all the excitement and overseas travel during December seemed to be a distant memory as Jade started her final year of high school. Being Deputy Head Girl, she had a lot of commitments and meetings. She also was playing field hockey, was in the school play, editor of the school newspaper and a top academic student.

At Kings Court, Simon was now in his first year of high school and a prefect as well as on the soccer and cricket team. He also participated in the school play. Time seemed to by flying by.

In the August of 1998, I was diagnosed with bladder cancer. I was devastated. It's amazing how things have a way of falling into perspective when one receives such news. I was firmly reassured by my specialist that I would be fine. After my first surgery, I spent four days in hospital and then had to have bed rest at home for another week. I was very spoiled by Terence and the children, and my friend Elizabeth came down to Tzaneen from Johannesburg for a few days to help out. Miriam could not give me enough cups of tea. Over the next few months, I would have to undergo a series of procedures to cauterize any other potentially developing tumors. I visited the hospital (situated in Pretoria, three and a half hours south of Tzaneen) every three months and thereafter every six months. Once all was clear, it would become a yearly visit.

We had made a weekend break on my first three month visit, booking in at a B&B near the hospital. I was feeling particularly nervous, so Terence took me and the children out for supper at a restaurant down the road from the B&B. We had a great meal, and I started to relax and not feel so anxious. We left the restaurant at about nine p.m. only to discover that our VW kombi had been stolen. We just could not believe it; we walked around the car park thinking that we might have parked in another bay. We were miles from home, surgery in the morning and no car. Most of our belongings were at the B&B except for our jackets, blankets and some shoes. The worst of all was Joffre's school suitcase, luckily it was early in the term as he had to re-write the books that were stolen, and the textbooks had to be re-purchased. The police took about two hours before they arrived as they were dealing with three other incidents of stolen cars in the same area. Once the police had left the restaurant the restaurateur gave us a lift to the B&B. We all had a very event filled night, only to get up early to prepare for the hospital.

I later found out that I should have told the anesthetist about the drama of the night before, and all the stress I was experiencing, as things could have become complicated and dangerous for me while under anesthesia. In the midst of all this I remembered Psalm 121 which I made my own on the day of my first surgery all those months ago. I opened up my bible that Terence had placed next to my bed and knew yet again the peace that surpasses all understanding. Once I had come around from the anesthetic Terence, and the children came and told me that they had a lift organized for us.

The young lady was Terence's boss's daughter who was living in Johannesburg at the time. She was going home to Duiwelskloof for the weekend to visit her family, and she was graciously willing to do a detour into Pretoria. All went well with the surgery, and by God's grace we were on our way home within the next few hours.

Life was moving on, Jade was in her final year of high school, and Joffre was in his first. We were still looking at leaving the country and heard about a job opportunity in the Seychelles. One of Jade's teachers had a brother that lived there, and we had organized a family holiday/job interview there for a week in October. We would be staying with her teacher's brother and family. Initially it was only going to be Terence and Joffre that would go, but Terence's mom and dad encouraged Jade and I to go. They felt it would be a good family break. Unfortunately, we did not have money for the extra two tickets. We had one of our cars for sale, an old blue Volkswagen Beetle, (Terence now had a company van) but no one was interested. We were going to use the money from that sale for our tickets. And if no one bought it, we would not go. We prayed but time was running out. If we were going to go with, we needed to book our tickets within the next week. With two days to go till our deadline, some friends from the church came over for lunch and a game of darts and saw the car was for sale. We did not have a set price and would be willing to negotiate on their offer. When they made the offer, it was the exact amount of money we needed for the extra air tickets — with some to spare! The Lord was truly good. I was delighted because if Terence was offered the job, I really wanted to see the island, the housing and the schooling before we moved there. I was feeling positive about the interview and extremely excited about seeing Seychelles.

Both children were at school, and I was out in the garden with Sarah when the call came, just to confirm that Terence was still coming over for the interview. In one week's, time we would be flying over the Indian Ocean to the incredibly beautiful Seychelles which are an archipelago of one hundred and fifty-eight islands in the Indian Ocean. It was located one thousand miles east, off the coast of Africa.

The pilot interrupted my daydreaming, "ladies and gentlemen please fasten your seat belts." Excitement mounted in me as I looked out of the small oval window to the turquoise beneath me. Once we landed and went through customs, we were met by the young family dad, mom and two young boys, we would stay with for the week. We met as strangers, but within half an hour were chatting like old friends. They drove us through the busy streets of Victoria, the capital of Mahé, the main island. I saw the Victorian clock in the middle of the main street, recognizing it from pictures I had seen in travel magazines. Winding our way up the mountain on the east side, we came across a daffodil yellow house with a green zinc roof. We were told by the youngest of the two boys that that was their house and where we would be staying. The house sat in a garden filled with trees and flowers and had the most amazing view. When stepping out of the front doors you were almost at the top of the world looking down onto the north side of the island. In the distance were Cerf Island and a few smaller islands jutting out from the tranquil and now very pink ocean as the sun set.

I was filled with awe and said a quick prayer of thanks, especially after everything that we as a family had gone through the past six years. I felt hope and peace and just glad to be healthy and alive. For the next seven days this world would be ours! The family that we were staying with had very busy work schedules, and their children were both at school all day. They were very kind and told us to treat their house like our own. They had given us the use of one of their cars which allowed us to be independent.

Terence had the interview the very next morning. We were up early, and the four of us left for the interview with me navigating a strange map — we made our way with lots of laughs through Victoria and to the industrial part of the town. The children and I sat in the car while Terence went in for the interview. He emerged an hour later with a look of despair. They were fairly friendly, but it was kind of like thanks for coming but no-thanks. We were both disappointed but had learned that doors shut for a reason. Oh well, at least we had the rest of the week to relax and enjoy the island.

We had so many adventures on that little island. We snorkeled in a protected marine park where we had to pay to use the beach — but it was totally worth it as we were the only people there. We met the local fishermen and women selling their catch of the day on the side of the road, just a few feet from the lapping waves where their boats bobbed up and down. And we spent a day on the main beach next to some not-so-modest honeymooners! The one thing that I will never forget was the day we went to Cerf Island, just a few kilometers off the coast of Mahé. Early one morning, our host and one of his sons took us on their small boat through the harbor dodging all the huge cruise-liners and tugboats. We were promised that it would be well worth the trip. And it certainly was…

Cerf Island is named after the French navy frigate "Le Cerf". Home to fruit bats, Clownfish and most famously the giant tortoise. The island lies in the Ste Anne Marine National Park and is surrounded by a coral reef. Here we ate toasted cheese sandwiches and drank ice cold cokes! The restaurant was literally on the beach and as we ate, we buried our toes into the restaurant floor — the beach sand.

Such a pity the job did not work out, I could have stayed there forever. All good things come to an end as they say, and we left for home a few days later.

1999 - 2000

Arriving back to South Africa really opened our eyes — even though it had only been a week, we had just felt so safe. We continued looking for jobs as the incidents of farm attacks in our area were becoming more and more. Terence was even witness to a gun fight in the middle of the street right outside the shop where he was working. Cash-in-transit heists were rife during this time. Robberies and murders on small business owners were very high on the list too. More common than not during this time. On more than one occasion Terence had gotten tips from the police saying that they would be staking out the shop that week as they had heard there was a hit on the shop and the workers. On those days when the police had been informed, they would send security to guard the shop and the employers as they cashed up at the end of the day. Terence's former business partner had been attacked and robbed. An attack on the shop was always at the back of our minds, we just had to keep praying and trusting God for Terence's safety and that of his co-workers.

After the second robbery at our own home, I decided with all seriousness that we needed to get out of that situation. I continued to look everywhere that the English language was spoken. There were lots of places offering the kinds of jobs Terence could do all over the world — though some of the places like Paris were inviting, our prerequisite would need it to be an English-speaking country. A foreign language is not always easy to learn, especially in the business world, and another thing was schooling for the children as they would come with us. For months night after night, I would stare tirelessly over the advertisements on the Internet to the point that my vision would start to blur. After a while when it seemed like there was nothing, I would slip back into the comfort zone of everyday life. I would get lazy and stop searching for jobs for months at a time. Then something would happen close to home — another break-in, another friend attacked, and I would get a bee in my bonnet, get myself geared and start the search yet again.

We had still heard nothing about our immigration application to the USA, and we had decided that that was no longer an option. It had been 10 years since we had first applied.

Jade had taken a year off to decide what she wanted to do, and in 2000 she started her first year at University of Pretoria for her bachelor's degree of science in zoology.

Joffre was doing very well at school excelling in sports like cricket and soccer. He also started a keen interest in golf and before long Terence was hooked, and we were spending weekends at the local country club playing rounds of golf.

2001 - 2002

Not finding anything overseas, I decided to start to look in South Africa. Advice from a friend led me to look more closely at the Cape Province. This time I had bought a newspaper called Job Mail. This was generally for jobs in South Africa, but a few overseas jobs were also advertised. I took her advice; it would be a good idea to move to the coast, maybe the ocean was what we all needed.

It was late one evening in January 2002. Terence had come home exhausted, he was working 12-14 hour shifts seven days a week, and we were now going into our tenth year. I started to go through the jobs page by page. At 11 p.m. after about four hours of searching, I had decided to call it a night. As I was closing the newspaper and placing it on the study desk, I noticed a small ad on the international page looking for an experienced retail manager for a supermarket in the Republic of Ireland. My heart skipped a beat. *How had I missed this ad?* I had read and re-read the paper for the past few days. Then and there, not waking Terence I turned on our computer and I waited for the dial-up to connect (the days before wireless). I found the website and applied on his behalf. Terence was very surprised when I told him the next morning, he laughed about it, thinking, *yeah right*. We had been trying for so long why not, let's just see what happens. Honestly, I had never even considered the Republic of Ireland. It was just a place I knew about. It was there — I was here. It was literally the last place I would have looked at.

A few days later, much to my delight and surprise, I received an e-mail from a lady in Durban who wanted a copy of Terence's resume. Within the next week an interview had been set up in Durban for Terence. Things suddenly seemed to have some momentum.

It was Thursday the 27th of February 2002. Joffre, Terence and I drove to Johannesburg. Jade was at university in Pretoria which was on the way to Johannesburg and so, we would pick her up on our way. We were staying with my friend Elizabeth in Randburg (a suburb of Johannesburg).

Friday morning the four of us got up early and together we all prayed about the interview. The interview was an hours' flight away. Terence would fly down in the morning and return from Durban that evening. Jade and Terence left as he would drive to the airport and she would take the car from there, go to her classes in Pretoria and then come back to Johannesburg in the afternoon. Elizabeth was working, so Joffre and I would stay at the apartment and hang out studying for his end of March exams. It seemed like the longest day ever and we watched the seconds tick by thinking, "okay Terence has landed in Durban, okay the interview is now, okay the interview is over" and then the phone rang! It was Terence, he just wanted to tell us that everything was fine, the interview had gone well and that he would tell us all in detail when we were all together. That evening we all met him at the airport. We were very curious to hear what happened and were talking non-stop. Excitement was building. Terence had gotten very positive feedback in the interview, and we just had to wait for the formality of the job acceptance from the supermarket owner in Ireland. I felt that things were coming together at last!

We then spent the rest of the weekend at Elizabeth's apartment in Johannesburg. On Sunday, we made our way back to Tzaneen dropping Jade off in Pretoria.

When we got back to Tzaneen it was business as usual, but there was something else this time, our potential immigration to Ireland. Every time the phone rang, I expected to hear from Ireland, every time I checked the e-mails my heart would quicken for just a second as I searched for an e-mail from Ireland — but nothing.

Maybe things had not gone as well as we thought? Maybe they had already filled the position from the EU countries? We just waited and prayed. It took about three weeks, and Terence received a call to say that he had got the job! It was finally happening. Our prayers had been answered. I remembered the bible verse from Romans 8:28 (NIV), "And we know that in all things God works for the good of those who love him, who have been called according to his purpose." My heart was at peace, a new adventure was on the horizon. We were told that it would still take another few months to get everything finalized from the Irish side, visas, work permits etc. This was great as we had a lot of our own preparations to finalize packing up our house, schooling etc. The excitement started to mount but nerves set in as well. I was not even sure what I was feeling at this point. It could have been 90 percent excited and 10 percent nerves or the other way around, I had no idea. All I knew, is that this is what we had dreamed of and prayed for, for years.

We had decided that the USA was out of the picture and that Ireland would be the place we were going to immigrate to and call our home. Joffre was in his final year at school (grade 12), and Jade was in her third year at university. God's timing was perfect yet again. We decided to take only the essentials with us. It was a major undertaking; we had so much personal stuff. Literally our entire lives of over one hundred years between us. We had birthday cards since the children were only a year old, Christmas cards and all the usual suspects when it comes to the sentimental things we all keep. I remember many evenings, sitting on the lounge floor with the children, filtering through boxes and deciding what we could take with us. Eventually, we had sentimental stuff which filled five trunks. We were also all only allowed one suitcase of 20 kilograms each.

As soon as we heard that Terence got the job in Ireland, we went to our friend and landlord to tell him the good news. We were planning on leaving at the end of the school year which was about another four months away. He was very supportive and reassured Terence that he would be there if we needed anything.

The last month that Terence was with us in South Africa became a bit of a blur there were so many people who wanted to say goodbye to him, old friends, new friends, church friends that organized farewell lunches, suppers, and braais (BBQs) and of course the logistic and legal side of things like bank accounts, policies, lawyers, police clearance certificates. On top of that organizing and packing up our entire household!

Terence left for Ireland on the 9th of September 2002, Jade was back at university and Joffre was preparing for his prelim exams. I got stuck in with the cleaning and packing with much help from Miriam. Towards the end, things were getting very busy and so we employed some extra help. Ester and Joseph who worked at our church and whom we knew well were only too willing to come and help. One day, Sarah did not arrive for work. I immediately thought the worst, however I heard via the "bush telegraph" she had found another job. I was relieved she was okay and perhaps had found it too sad to say goodbye.

Most of our belongings were sold, and some of the more sentimental items were given to friends and family. Needless to say, Miriam got the bulk of our stuff as she had been part of the family for so long.

Because we had to sell our car in preparation for the immigration, a friend of ours had a car that he was not using, and we were then able to use it for the duration of our stay which was a wonderful blessing.

The 27th of September 2002 dawned cool with a chance of rain.

Today was the day that I was going to euthanize our three dogs. Over the course of the years living on the farm we had a few dogs and two cats. Unfortunately, some of the dogs and the two cats had passed on. So, the dogs that we had left were a German Sheppard, a Scotty and a mongrel from the back of the shop were Terence used to work. This decision we had discussed and made when we had first applied for immigration many years ago. That no matter what animals we had, they would not be given away to anyone, but they would be euthanized.

On that day, I made sure that Jade and Joffre were not at home, and they went out with friends for the day. At about ten a.m. the vet came out to the farm to see to the animals which was great because normally you would have to take the animals to the vet's offices but because of the situation we were in he had said that he would come out and help me at home.

He was first going to sedate the dogs and then put them to sleep. Our one dog, Mac the mongrel was not happy. They have that sixth sense, and he knew that something was not right. He bit the vet on the hand, and we realized that the sedation was not strong enough. It seemed like he was fighting for his life, like he knew what was about to happen. The vet had to drive back into town to get some more sedation medicine which left me once again with the dogs just waiting, dreading the time to come. He came back at 11:30 a.m., together we sedated the dogs, and then in turn we went to each one and put them to sleep. Euthanizing a healthy animal was just devastating, but in my heart I just knew it was the right thing to do. I could never have left them behind; I would always wonder what was happening to them. Were they being cared for? Were they missing us? Were they waiting for us? Mac hated lightning, and I would never have known if the person would have kept him outside during storms. I could not live with myself knowing that these things might have happened.

Joseph had dug an enormous mass grave on the side of the house. The vet waited until after the dogs had died. He then helped me carry them out, and we laid them in the grave. He turned to me and asked if I was okay. I said that I was, putting on a brave face, even though this was the furthest thing from the truth. He left about 1:30 p.m.

Once he left, I went outside and picked a handful of the most beautiful purple iris and violets we had growing in the garden. I laid them in the grave with the dogs and slowly started to fill the grave. Joseph was going to come back later that afternoon and fix the grave properly as it was hard work to shovel the soil, and I was really not up to it at this point. I just went back inside and cried for what seemed like hours. I then made myself a strong cup of coffee and realized the best thing to do was to keep myself busy as there was still so much to do.

That evening Jade, Joffre, and I stayed with our friends James and Melissa who lived and worked on the Sapeko tea estates. The estate was on top of a hill overlooking the valley with Tzaneen in the distance. James and Melissa were wonderful, and they treated us to KFC and tried to make a little light of the day considering all that we had been through. We would be staying with them from now on until we left for Ireland.

Our house in Tzaneen was completely empty. Everything was gone. We had very little to do, and the final steps of cleaning the windows and tidying up the garden were things that I would drive down to the valley to do.

On the 1st of October, I went back down into the valley. I took our landlord our final month of rent and to say a final goodbye. I spent the morning with him and his wife having tea accompanied by delicious rock buns and meringues, which their housekeeper was famous for. They were very sad to see us go and yet were so supportive in their words about our future.

On my way back to James and Melissa, I stopped at our house one last time. I said a fond farewell to the house that took us in when we needed it most and looked at it as a house of healing. We had arrived at a house as a very sad and unsettled family and left a home with lots of great memories. I stood and looked at the garden which Sarah and I had developed, the flowers, the trees, and the large expanse of lawn where we had played and had so much fun. The beautiful dam in the distance where our dear hippopotamus lived and who used to visit us every now and again; where the children had so much fun on their tractor tubes; where we fished and found an old raft. I will never forget the way the dogs would run and swim as we all played in the water. It all came back to me as I stood and looked out. Lastly, I went to the dog's grave and said a final goodbye. I could not stay any longer; I could feel the tears welling up.

I remember
South African days
South African nights
Times in the sun, times in the heat
The nights are cool, and the rains have come
I remember your name

Standing surrounded by the past and thinking of the future and what lay ahead. I was overwhelmed. Without looking back, I got into the car and drove away.

Our three month stay with James and Melissa was wonderful. They are truly the kind of people that mean it when they say, "Our home is your home". They had two sons who had already left home. This worked for us as it meant that Joffre and I each got our own room. Each evening we would all take a slow walk through the tea plantation. The adults would walk while Joffre and sometimes James would jog; it was always the same route every evening. Their dog, Jess, a dear old black Labrador would be between the four of us. After returning from our walks, James and Joffre would sometimes play darts on the back porch. We would all end up sitting and chatting outside as the summer evenings were getting longer, and it was extremely pleasant with the house very high up on top of the mountain looking out onto a lake and the tea plantation that was world renowned.

Time went by so quickly, and Joffre and Jade both had finals coming up. Jade was coming home less, and Joffre was spending the majority of his time studying for his final school exams. On his study breaks, he spent time with friends fishing and generally hanging out knowing this would be the last summer he would have with them. James and Melissa had full time jobs and so I was at home alone most of the time. I was at a loose end as I did not have my own home anymore, I had very little to do and so with permission from James and Melissa, their gardener and I started to re-landscape their garden. Their housekeeper was extremely proud of her work and would not let anyone do any housework or help in the house, so I was in the garden.

We all missed Terence terribly. We spoke at least once a week as well as a weekly letter from me and some little inspirational cards, Bible verses etc to keep his chin up. He was struggling in Ireland on his own, so I just felt that a letter every week from the children and I would help.

During October and November, Joffre wrote his finals and had his matric farewell. When Jade came home after her finals in mid-November, Joffre's exams had just ended, and we went around saying our goodbyes. We had so many teas, cakes, and the occasional braai, our friends were so generous, and we got the nicest farewell gifts to send us on our way.

On the 27th of November, we got up early as this was the day we were leaving South Africa for good. James and Melissa were very kindly going to take us up to Johannesburg. They had a small truck and a trailer filled to the brim with all our suitcases as well as James and Melissa's weekend luggage and loads of fresh fruit bought at one of the local fruit vendors on the side of the road for their family in the city. We were going to stay with Elizabeth for a few days while we waited for our flight to Ireland on the 2nd of December 2002. I also had to have my last cancer check-ups at the hospital in Pretoria which was en-route to Johannesburg. We ate

McDonalds on the rooftop of the hospital, and a friend of Jade's joined us. What made everything so much better was that my last test was clear, and all was fine.

Later that afternoon, we arrived at Elizabeth's townhouse. Three days later, friends and family gathered at Johannesburg International Airport to say their goodbyes. I still remember as we turned back to wave for the last time, Terence's late dad filming us on his video camera and his mom holding back her tears.

PART TWO

THE REPUBLIC OF IRELAND

2002 - 2003

We flew from South Africa to Madrid where we had a layover and then caught a connecting flight to Dublin.

We were welcomed in Dublin by wonderful Irish weather, rain. It was freezing so all the jackets and jerseys came in really useful.

We did have a problem when we came into customs. The Irish customs had previous problems with South African passport holders. So, the three of us and four young men that were going over for Rugby training were detained. We were detained and questioned for about 45 minutes, and I was getting really concerned. They were re-asking all the questions and checking and re-checking all our paperwork. They even called the supermarket where Terence was working. They did a lot of extra questioning with the young rugby players who were still being detained when we were free to go. I gave them Terence's cell number and told them to contact us if they needed anything. (About an hour later they called to let me know they were fine and on their way to Athlone.) Meanwhile, Terence was still upstairs waiting for us knowing that the plane had landed, but with no idea as to where we were, he was getting a little anxious. All sorts of things crossed his mind like had we missed our flight? Were we safe? Eventually, we were reunited after three months, and it was wonderful. There were hugs and kisses all around.

We were then introduced to Tom and his young son Kevin that had come up to Dublin with Terence to help take all our luggage back. Our little car that Terence had bought, the little tomato red Toyota Corolla, was tiny and basically just fit the four of us and our hand luggage.

Tom was a member of the Baptist church that Terence had joined. The church had very generously given Tom and Terence the petrol money for the trip to Dublin. We left the airport and started to travel back to Ballaghaderreen which was about three hours West across Ireland. At the halfway point of the journey we stopped at a little restaurant which was buzzing with people. It was still freezing, and the warmth of the restaurant was very welcoming. It would be the first taste of Irish food, and I must say that we were quite impressed and delighted especially with the soup which we continue to still talk about to this day.

After about an hour, Tom and Kevin graciously left the restaurant and headed home, giving our family time alone to catch up. You do not think that so much can happen in three months, but it does. Terence then took a slower and more scenic drive home. Being the middle of winter, everything was grey and bleak but for me it held a beauty of its own. It was a great drive, and I can still remember it in detail, best of all my family was all together.

Later that afternoon, we pulled into the small driveway that led up to our new home. I could see the warm lights through the windows as some of the church folk had turned on the lights and central heating so that it was prepared for our warm homecoming. I immediately fell in love with the house, it was a far cry from the African farmhouse we had come to love but held a somewhat fairy-tale charm. It was a semi-detached up and down stairs in the newer part of town, painted in a soft yellow. The small garden in the back had grass knee high and the front had a postage size piece of lawn.

We entered the house and as well as being warm it smelled delicious. It turned out some of the church ladies had also generously left us dinner in the oven. We also had another surprise when we found our luggage neatly stacked in the hallway.

The supermarket owner organized a work permit for Jade and Joffre for the coming year. I, being Terence's spouse, shared his. We all started to work about two weeks after our arrival. I worked in the milk fridges which was horrendous. I was coming from a 40-degree Celsius summer into a minus degree winter, and now I was in the fridges! It was so cold that the skin on my hands started to peel, and I went through an amazing number of gloves. Joffre and Terence both got their forklift licenses, and the one lady that worked in the cool drink isle retired, so Joffre took over from her. Jade worked upstairs in the office. One evening, while we were getting ready to close the shop for the day, a very bedraggle, sad, wet, and cold little white kitten scurried into the shop.

No matter how many times one of the store associates put it outside it kept coming back in. Eventually, the supermarket staff persuaded us (with very little persuasion, I might add) to adopt the little kitten. That evening, we left home with a very scared kitten and all that goes with it. That evening we discovered two things about our new pet, he was a tomcat and he was stone deaf. We called him Joshua. He was pure white and had the most beautiful eyes — one green and one blue. We taught him a self-invented sign language, and he responded so wonderfully and naturally. We would never sneak up on him to get his attention. We would gently touch his head to let him know that we were there. His favorite place to sleep was in the clothes dryer after the warm, dry clothes had been removed. By mid December the main street had been adorned with white Christmas lights that had been strung across the streets from building to building. The traditional Christmas tree had been erected in the main square at the top of Main Street. We attended the turning on of the lights with the rest of the towns-folk. Even though it was below freezing and raining this did not deter the festive mood of all the people. One of my most favorite things was walking down the main street in the evenings. The Christmas lights reflecting on the wet streets and pavements while the cathedral clock played a Christmas carol each time the clock struck on the hour. I clearly remember hearing the bell toll "The First Noel". The smell of peat fires filled the cold, frosty air always leaving me with a feeling of belonging.

On the 23rd of December, the supermarket owner gave us a fresh Christmas tree, a string of colored lights and a potted holly bush. Our trunk was loaded with festive foods including a 20lb turkey. This was totally foreign for us. Since we had been married Terence had worked every Christmas and now a few days off, what a treat! I bought a small Christmas wreath and hung it on the front door. It was our first winter Christmas. On the evening of the 24th of December, we were invited to a Christmas Eve mass at a hundred-year-old abbey/convent just out of town. This would be the last mass held there as it had been sold to developers who were going to turn it into a hotel. The few elderly nuns that were living there were moving to Dublin. It was a lovely service. Afterwards, we drank tea and ate cake and mince pies in the old kitchen. Later, we sat around a piano in the lounge and sang Christmas carols.

The few days following Christmas, I just wanted to explore. Terence and I would take long walks no matter the weather around Ballaghaderreen. Our most common walk and the most popular with the locals was through the fields and past the piggery. We would often pass farmers with their dogs as well as other locals. I would often come home frozen but exhilarated and relax in front of our fireplace! I loved my new home and its surroundings.

Ireland
I feel the wind, on an Irish winter's day
Feeling the cold throughout my bones
The fireplace is what I need
A good book and a cup of tea

At the end of January, Jade wanted to go back to South Africa to complete her zoological and genetics degree. We suggested her doing it in Galway, but she preferred to go back to her old university. She left at the end of February. We were already looking forward to the summer when she would be home for her break. Terence, Joffre and I continued to live and work in Ballaghaderreen making a new life for ourselves.

I could not believe that it was already March and with it St. Patrick's Day! The atmosphere was electric as the townsfolk lined Main Street of Ballaghaderreen to watch the St. Patrick's Day parade. It was a perfect day the sun peeked from behind the clouds and the rain stayed away. The color of the day was definitely green, and even if you weren't Irish you felt like you belonged to the Emerald Isle. As the floats, musicians and dancers left the town hall and made their way down Main Street, the cheering and clapping was deafening. We all waved our Irish flags singing along with the tunes as they floated on the air. The parade made its way towards the majestic cathedral, it's destination for the day. Some folks stood around chatting after the parade while others strolled to their favorite pub for a famous glass of Guinness.

An Ireland we are called
The calling we make
Shoulder to shoulder
United we stand

As Terence, Joffre and I left Main Street Joffre complained of a sharp pain in his right side. By the time we reached the car Joffre was doubled up with pain. We were advised to drive Joffre to the hospital in Sligo, little did we realize how much of a detour we would have to take. Certain streets were closed due to the St. Patrick's Day parade but with much twisting and turning we eventually arrived at the hospital.

The waiting room in the hospital was fairly full, and we were told that they would be dealing with emergency cases first. Joffre's pain was acute but still bearable, so we had to wait our turn. A young boy who had fallen off a ladder and had broken his arm was next to be seen. His sobs of pain could be heard as he was led down a passage, and then it was Joffre's turn. The doctor that attended Joffre was concerned about his appendix. It was, he described as a "rumbling appendix." For further treatment, observation was the result. Our St. Patrick's Day plans were put on hold. On the second day, we met with the doctor to hear the result of the observation treatment. We were told his pain had receded and that he would be discharged once the surgeon general had made his rounds. Included in the treatment were several injections to the affected areas which Joffre remembers to this day. This was certainly a St. Patrick's Day the three of us would always remember.

With the days growing longer, Terence and Joffre took full advantage of playing golf. I would sometimes go with them but on most occasions stay home writing letters to friends and family and just enjoying my new home.

At every opportunity, we headed out exploring; we were given maps and sometimes directions by the local pub owner whose pub was semi-attached to the supermarket. A very friendly, upbeat local who had the wonderful gift of storytelling. Most Monday mornings he would be waiting outside the back entrance of the pub to hear where we had been. Later in the week I would show him photos I had taken of all the places we had been. I was using a small Kodak instamatic camera that my father-in-law had given me after he used it on a previous trip to the States. It became part of our lives for many years to come.

A few Saturday mornings, I helped at a non-kill dog shelter where I met the most amazing people. I would drive the ten kilometers through the countryside, which was changing as the spring arrived. Seeing the wild daffodils reminded me of one of the poems I learned at school by William Wordsworth called "Daffodils". Their perfect yellow faces watching me as I drove past them. The Gorse bushes covered the landscape as if someone had spilt huge pots of yellow paint. On one occasion, I stopped the car in the middle of nowhere and picked tall pink wild lupines. This was a new concept for me as in South Africa I would never have left an open car parked at the side of a country road, let alone wander around picking flowers on my own. As spring gently moved into summer, window boxes and baskets attached to the lamp posts billowed with the most colorful flowers imaginable.

Irish eyes
Face to face
Do not blink
On this Irish day

During the summer months, we spent most of our weekends sight-seeing and exploring Ireland. We would leave early in the morning and would only return early evenings. We would travel all over sometimes locally and sometimes between fifty to one hundred miles per trip, seeing some of the most amazing scenery that simply took our breath away.

One of my most memorable trips was to Lough Key Forest near Carrick on Shannon. The lough was surrounded by lush grass and beautiful trees. To one side of the lough was a forest that was filled with bluebells as far as the eye can see. As we walked deeper into the forest we came across a beautiful old grey stoned bridge called the Fairy Bridge. As we crossed the bridge it was like we entered a magical kingdom with a huge chair in the middle of the bluebells made from the same grey stones as the bridge, called the Wishing Chair. It felt like we had gone back in time as we stood under the canopy of the trees.

Two of our trips took us through Yeats country, an area dedicat-ed to the poet Yeats. We found the Yeats Country Inn Restaurant and Hotel. During our many meandering trips, we would often stop and have a tasty meal at the restaurant which never disap-pointed.

We also spent a wonderful day at Ashford Castle and park which is near Cong in County Mayo-Galway border. Walking around the gardens was so peaceful, the flowers of every color were so vivid one could not imagine how grey and bleak Ireland was in the winter months. Later that day, we had a meal at the local pub in Cong. The 1952 movie *The Quiet Man* with John Wayne and Maureen O' Hara was filmed in this area and is still know as 'Quiet Man Country' by some people.

A visit to the cliffs of Moher is a must, located at the edge of the Burren in County Clare. As we walked along the cliffs, we could smell the sea on the very cold breeze as the waves constantly battered the sides of the cliffs where the cheeky, beautiful colorful Puffins nested. Staring out onto the Atlantic Ocean is just mesmerizing. We left cold and damp but in such awe of these magnificent cliffs.

Green green
This is Ireland
Land of the green
Green green
For all to see
From the north to south
From east to west
The famous two words
Green green

We also visited The National Museum of Ireland Life which is situated near Castlebar in County Mayo, exploring and learning the fascinating culture and traditions of old Ireland. Striking black and white photographs adorned the walls, each telling their own story. A great setting for a step back in time!

As we were settling into Irish life, Joshua was very quickly getting used to being an indoor cat. He would still occasionally venture outside and so because he was deaf, we bought him a little collar with a bell so that we knew where he was at all times. One evening, he went exploring in the back garden but had somehow found his way into the road in front of our house and was hit by a car. We tried to get him to a vet but unfortunately his injuries were so severe he passed away in the car halfway to the vet. We were all devastated, and we will all always have a place in our hearts for our little Irish cat.

In the middle of July, we were contacted to say that our green cards had been approved. We were shocked! We applied in 1991 this was 2003 and we had only one letter from the United States Immigration in all that time. The one big, very big problem was that Jade had aged out which meant she was not issued a green card. Since we (her whole family) would be in the USA, we figured that it would be a fairly easy and prompt process for a green card to be issued to her. If the paperwork took a few months longer than we expected, we still had the holidays to look forward to when Jade could come for a visit. All we had to do was to re-apply for her as our daughter once we arrived in the USA.

I was torn in two, leaving Ireland after just settling down or going to the United States, our first choice. Terence was keen to go as were both Jade and Joffre; I was very much on the fence. Staying in Ireland could be a possibility for us, but we would have to apply for new work permits every year up until we could apply for Irish citizenship, a process that could be four or more years. We spoke to local garda in Ballaghaderreen who said since the European Union (EU) passport holders were streaming into Ireland, and they did not need a work permit, this could be a hindrance to us, as our Irish work permits might not be re-issued. He felt we shouldn't take the chance. We prayed and discussed the matters that lay before us especially Jade's future. No decision was taken lightly.

We would have permanent residency in the USA, no guarantees in Ireland and nothing to go back to in South Africa.

In September, we once again had our five trunks collected for shipping this time to the United States. The friends I had made at the dog shelter gave us a wonderful farewell party. Our church friends were very upset we were leaving but understood our predicament. I took photos of virtually the whole town; even the most camera-shy people were willing to pose. All the employees at the supermarket, who in the beginning were skeptical of us, shed tears on the day we left. We had arrived as foreigners from Africa and left as 'honoree Irish'.

Dancing and singing, that's what we do
We sing, we dance and we drink in the pub
A friendly smile, greetings to all
The home of the green is Ireland

PART THREE

THE REPUBLIC OF SOUTH AFRICA

2003 - 2004

We left Ireland in late September as we had to go back to South Africa in order to start our immigration process. We had arranged to stay with Terence's brother Brian and his daughter May-Lin. My in-laws, who were still living with Brian, were visiting the Ruth at the time we were in South Africa, so Terence and I would be using their room while Jade and Joffre would sleep on mattresses on the floor of Brian's TV/games room.

Witbank is about a two hours' drive from Johannesburg, where the United States Consulate was. Brian had two vehicles, one he used daily for work and another was a restored bright, red Volkswagen Beetle he allowed us to use.

Some of Jade's friends lived on the same street as Brian, and just before her final exams started, she got a ride to Witbank with them and surprised us with a weekend visit! It was so special having my whole family together again under one roof. We spent the weekend catching up on so much stuff. It would only be a month and a half till we would see her again as she would be writing her final exams to complete her degree.

Time was moving so fast I could not believe it was already the end of October. On Halloween, May-Lin encouraged us to dress up; we had never celebrated Halloween (it was not very celebrated in South Africa), but we decided that as a family we would dress up and have some fun!

No one would be ringing our doorbells, and no one would be trick-or-treating, but by putting our heads together and raiding all the cupboards in the house we came up with some really good costumes. His youngest daughter, Jocelyn, lived with her mom on the South Coast of Kwazulu-Natal and spent a holiday with us. We got to know the girls really well; we had always lived far from each other only spending a few days together on Easter and Christmas, so it was nice getting to spend some quality time with them.

During the first week in November, Jade wrote her final exam for her final year. We drove up to Pretoria (about an hour away) to pick up Jade from university. We arrived at the residence where Jade had been for the last four years, home away from home. There was organized chaos as we pulled up outside the building finding a parking spot under one of the thousands of Jacaranda trees that lined the streets of Pretoria also known as Jacaranda City. There were young women hauling suitcases, boxes, and clothes still draped on hangers spilling out of the building. Jade was all packed and ready to go. She was waiting for us next to her residences' beloved mascots, two majestic cement yellow lions that guarded the entrance. We managed to load Jade's goodies into the VW Beetle dividing it between the boot and the back seat around which Jade and I sat. Goodbyes were said a bittersweet moment as we pulled away for the last time. Before heading out on the highway, we stopped for take away hamburgers and chips which we ate on our way home. Our family was once more together, I gave up grateful thanks. It was difficult being so far away from one of my children. Halfway back to Brian's we became aware of a funny sound coming from the front right wheel, it did not sound good. We were now on the highway and all prayed that we did not break down as we were in a hijacking hot spot. It was a sad sight to see that since we had been away the South African government had posted signs along the busy highways in South Africa where hi-jackings had been known to have occurred. There was no solution to the problem except to make the travelers aware and put up a sign with a big exclamation mark and the words "Hi-Jacking Hot Spot", warning people not to stop. It was so surreal compared to living in Ireland where we never even locked our car. Eventually, we pulled into Brian's driveway safe and sound, sadly, that was the first and last trip we made in the Beetle it just would not budge. After finding out that it had major engine failure and financially it would have cost too much to fix, Brian decided to sell it.

Luckily, the shops were in walking distance and on the weekend we would go with Brian to do a big shop, go to the movies or just visit the mall.

There was a lot of paperwork that had to get done. We had no idea how long we would have to wait for our interview but with the holidays coming up and knowing that most government offices closed for two weeks, we had no time to waste. Terence, Joffre and I had to get police clearance certificates. Joffre and I could use the ones we obtained before going to Ireland as we had not been there for a full year. Terence had obtained his police clearance from the garda in Ballaghaderreen before we left.

The United States Immigration Department had provided us with a list of approved physicians that we needed to go and see in order to get our medical clearance certificates. At this time there were only three approved physicians in the whole country. Once again, we had the favor of the Lord, and the one physician was at a large hospital in Pretoria. The physician could have been in another city or province which would have meant a long drive or a flight with an overnight stay. Terence, Joffre and I had to have a full physical exam as well as chest X-Rays to make sure we did not have TB. We also had to have certain vaccinations one of which was tetanus. The whole process took a few hours as we went from one area in the hospital to another. We had a long wait while our x-rays were developed and all paperwork to be re-checked. Eventually, we left the hospital each clutching a huge sealed envelope full of test results and X-Rays. These would have to remain sealed until we landed at our port of entry, where they would open them and then and there decide if we would be allowed to stay or had to catch the next flight back to SA.

We finally had all of our paperwork, and now to wait for our interview date. I was getting rather excited as the thing we had been waiting for was so close. We had decided that Jade would come with us to the U.S. Consulate, and she would apply for a visitor's visa so that we could all go over together. Once we were there; we could chat to our immigration lawyer on the status of her green card. We were all going to be together, and we were going to have Christmas in the United States!

The day of our long awaited interview at the U.S. Consulate in Johannesburg was finally here. It was a beautiful morning with a cool breeze in the air, and I felt hope rise in me as we all piled into Brian's car. The two hour drive was mostly silent. Everyone felt a bit nervous but mostly excited about what our new lives would bring. We had planned to start looking for air-tickets as soon as we got back to Witbank.

We arrived half an hour early for the visit.

The security line for the consulate started on the outside of the building and it's huge wall, on the sidewalk. Luckily, there were some trees as it was now starting to get hot. There were about twenty people in line all waiting to get a visa for one reason or another. All of us stood chatting for a little while until the gates opened and a consulate official stepped out of the consulate. He was very stern, and he started to walk the line asking everyone for their reason for coming to the consulate. You had to have your letter with you and your receipt for your visit. Every time you had an appointment for any kind of visa at the consulate there was a non-refundable fee that you had to pay whether you were granted your visa or not. The officer never smiled, and his face showed absolutely no expression. Security was understandably tight. It had only been two years since attacks on the 11th of September 2001. Needless to say, after that everyone was a little quieter as everyone started checking their paperwork again and then stood in silence.

We had one of the first morning appointments and once the doors opened, we all filed into the lobby where our first security check would commence. We had to hand in all cell phones, keys and any other electronic devices. We were physically searched and had to step through a metal detector. Once again, all officials were very strict, unemotional and just barked instructions at all of us. I had never experienced anything like this before and was starting to get a little nervous.

Once we had passed through security, we were ushered in a larger room. On the left hand side were multiple cubicles with bullet proof glass and a phone attached to the wall. On the right hand side of the room there were rows of brown hard chairs. The carpets were brown, and the walls were grey and empty. The room was cold and uninviting, and the air-conditioner was so low that everyone reached for a sweater as they took their seats. There was a nervous tension in the room, and the only noise was muffled voices and the fluttering of papers. Terence kept checking and re-checking that we had everything that was required.

The first five names were called, and each person got up and went to the cubical assigned to them. Jade was one of them. Those applying for visitors' visas had to go to the cubicles on the left and those who were immigrating had to go to the cubicles on the right.

After about ten minutes, she looked at us and shook her head — she was denied. She also could not stay with us and wait and had to leave the consulate immediately after her interview. She went and sat in the car with Brian, and they both waited for us.

As she walked out my heart ached a little because we would not be able to see our new home and our new lives together. My thoughts were quickly interrupted by the crying of a young lady. She rushed past us with tears streaming down her face. I remembered talking to her outside. She had been engaged to an American, and they were about to get married. She was planning a visit to go and see him and meet his family. I am not sure what took place during her interview, but I thought to myself, *"surely it can't be that bad"*.

I was wrong.

A few seconds later our names were called and Terence, Joffre and I headed to the second cubical on the right. We greeted the consular officer with a friendly good morning only to be greeted with a curt nod of his head and no eye contact. He then told us to slip our papers under the bullet-proof glass.

He started to go through all of our documents. He divided them up, some to the left and some to the right. I started to feel sick. He never spoke to us or even looked up at us for at least ten minutes.

After what seemed like an eternity, he looked up at us and very sarcastically said that I had forgotten to sign one of the forms. No worries I could just sign it now. He then said that Terence needed a police clearance from Dublin, not Ballaghaderreen. We also needed to get a new marriage certificate, an unabridged version. He told me that I needed to sign the one paper I had missed and until I had he would not help us. He then put all the papers back in a messy pile and literally flung them through the gap with an arrogant and dismissive toss of his hand. He immediately turned his back on us and picked up the conversation he was having with one of his colleagues. The papers fell on the floor, and as I was picking them up, I started looking for the one that I needed to sign. Tears pricked my eyes, but I would not give him the satisfaction of seeing he had upset me. I found the paper I needed and signed it as Terence picked up the other papers off the floor and started to organize them neatly again.

With the signed paper in my hand and not wanting to antagonize him anymore I just stood waiting for him to finish his conversation upon which he just motioned us back to the window with his finger. We stepped forward, and he told us that we had to have a written and oral test to once again determine our English language skills. We also had to come back in two weeks with correct police clearance and marriage certificate. We were dismissed. I was in total shock and needless to say the drive back to Witbank was silent. All of us trying to understand what had just happened. We had never been treated to badly. I was beginning to second guess our decision to move to the USA.

Due to the time difference we had to wake up very early the next morning to call the Dublin police and explain the situation to them. The police officer explained that this was unprecedented due to the fact that they do not issue police clearance to residence from another town. This had to be issued by the garda from your local town where you had lived, the garda that knew you. We said thank you and hung up. I guess we would have to try and explain that to the next consular officer. Perhaps they would be a little more understanding. The rest of the house was still asleep, so I made Terence and I some coffee, and we sat in the bedroom and wondered if we were doing the right thing. I was starting to have doubts. Should we go back to Ireland? Should we just stay in South Africa?

Terence was always so positive and told me that everything happens for a reason (one of his dad's favorite quotes) and that everything will work out.

Later that morning we drove to the South African Department of Home Affairs. Brian was getting rides to work, so we could generously use his car. It was so opposite to our experience the day before.

The lobby was painted green and stood empty. Thank goodness we had come early as there was no one there. Home Affairs visits could literally take you the whole day, as it is a first come first serve system and depends on what you are going for. There was also usually a wait time of six to twelve weeks for any paperwork. We only had two weeks. I said a silent prayer as we walked into the main waiting room. The lobby had been the calm before the storm. The large room was packed and stacked with people waiting to see an official. There were ladies feeding their babies, there were men standing talking and laughing, there were children playing on the floor and then there was us. Terence, Joffre and I the only three white people in the room. The room was hot and humid, and even with the intolerable heat everyone was patient just waiting their turn which was such a difference to the day before. There was no place to even sit in the waiting area and there were already long lines at each counter. Each counter had one official behind it and two chairs where the visitors would sit and talk to the officials. We stood against the wall trying to figure out which line we had to stand in. We asked an official who was walking by, and he politely pointed to a lady sitting behind one of the counters. Her line only had two other people in it, and so we went and stood in line.

After a few minutes we were called to her desk. She looked up at us and smiled and asked how she could help us. We explained our situation and she offered us two chairs while she went to the back to see how she could help us. As she left, I looked at Terence and smiled, he was right it would all be okay. She emerged with some documents we needed to fill out. She knew we were on a very tight deadline and said she would do whatever she could to help us out. We chatted about general things for a few minutes and then we left.

What a difference that visit was compared to the rudeness and arrogance of our consulate officer. It seemed so ironic to me that the country we were leaving was treating us so well, and the country that was opening their doors to us was so rude and cold. I left Home Affairs feeling a little lighter in my spirit. It was good to know that there were still people in this world willing to help their fellow man.

December in Witbank can be extremely hot bringing thunderstorms in the late afternoon. The huge white billowing clouds bulking up from about lunch time, by late afternoon the sky was grey and foreboding. Lightning shooting from one end of the sky to the other, the wind sings through the trees, rain pours down leaving the earth refreshed and smelling sweet. Normally by evening the sky has cleared and the stars twinkle from a black canvas. We spent some lovely summer evenings braaing and eating under the stars. We would set up a table in the back garden, Brian is a master at braaing, so he would be chief meat and chicken chef. Jade, May-Lin and I would prepare the rest of the meal in the kitchen normally with veggies, salads and bread warmed in the oven. Terence and Joffre would set up the chairs and tables under the big Arcadia tree. We would pick fresh flowers from the garden, mainly Agapanthus, as center pieces for the table. We would gather around and hold hands and say grace. Thankful to be together for this short time. I so enjoyed the warm weather and eating outside, something we did not do in Ireland. All the while in the back of my mind would be the question — how long would we be here for and when we left how long would it be before Jade would be able to join us in the United States?

The following week all government offices, as we thought, would be closed for two weeks and this included the U.S. Consulate. We would have to wait for the new year for our second interview visit. Christmas was just around the corner, so Jade and I decided to make it a special one since we had no idea when we would be able to celebrate together again. Brian was not much into decorating for Christmas so with his permission we raided the garage finding some rather old and battered Christmas decorations as well as a small fake Christmas tree. Joffre's birthday was just a few days before Christmas, so he got to have them as his birthday décor as well. Joffre's choice of meal for his birthday was KFC, one of Joffre's favorite meals, followed by his birthday cake I had baked the night before decorating it with smarties in the shape of a "20". We all had a wonderful afternoon, by the time we sang happy birthday and cut the cake we were all feeling much happier and relaxed than we had been in weeks. That evening we sat around the dining room table with old photos from when Brian and Terence were young and growing up in Tzaneen.

It was a wonderful evening of reminiscing and much laughter. It was so hard to believe that exactly a year ago, to the date we were experiencing our first Irish Christmas party dancing the night away to a local band playing good old rock and roll the lead singer fancying himself as Elvis. During the meal everyone raised their glasses singing happy birthday to Joffre what a wonderful way to celebrate your first "Irish" birthday.

2004

By now it was the 10th of January 2004, we were just waiting for our second interview when we received our unabridged marriage certificate in the mail! Wow! What a miracle. And there was the Christmas holiday that could have delayed the process. God had provided ours before our second interview. This was the only piece of paper we needed. The interview date loomed, and I remember I hardly slept the night before. The next morning, we drove up from Witbank, it felt like déjà vu, same drive, same security line, same cold waiting room, and my stomach was in knots. We sat in the same chairs and waited to be called to the small bulletproof glass window. This time we saw a different official. I said a silent prayer; this one is bound to be better than the first. I was wrong… same cold, arrogant and unfriendly manner. We explained that on our first visit we were told to get the unabridged marriage certificate and a criminal clearance certificate from Dublin and then to come back. We handed him our marriage certificate and explained that Dublin does not issue Criminal Clearance Certificates for people that have not lived in Dublin and that only the local garda can do that. He eyed us with what seemed like suspicion as if we were lying, and then he started going through all of our paperwork. I was so nervous, with every flip of his fingers through our papers my heart raced.

He then, without saying a word to us, got up and walked away and spoke to another official behind one of the desks. We just stood and looked at each other, each of us with a feeling of dread in the pit of our stomachs.

After about five minutes, he came back to the window, he shoved our paperwork back at us under the glass and told us that our three green cards had been sent back to the USA.

What? Why would they do that? Had they been revoked? What now? So many questions raced through our minds as we stood there speechless! I could not understand; they had made the appointment for us to come back and see them?

Terence was as patient as any man could be and without wanting to provoke the official asked why they had been sent back even though we had been given the time and date when to collect them.

The official just rolled his eyes and stated very matter-of-factly that visas are not kept at the consulate. If they were not issued within a certain time they were sent back to the USA. With that, he waved us away and called for the next visitor.

Our minds were in turmoil. What do we do now? This was completely out of hand. At this point I was even debating if this was a country I wanted to move to. We just had to have faith and trust God's timing.

We drove back to Brian's house in silence. By this time, we were ready to shelve the whole American dream. This fiasco was costing us a lot of money. None of us were working and time was ticking by. We were going into our fourth month of waiting. That night we prayed earnestly asking God, once again, if this was truly what He wanted for us and our future. There was nothing more we could do, it was in God's hands. A few days later, we received a phone call from a consular officer to tell us all the issues with our paperwork had been resolved and our visas were ready.

Terence could pick them up as soon as the following day and that Joffre and myself did not even have to be present. Once again, we made plans to drive up to the consulate. The lady that called from the consulate was surprisingly friendly and chatty, a real turnaround from the rude officers we had been dealing with. Our prayers had been answered.

Once we had our visas, we were ready to look for flights to the United States. By now I did not want to go. I would have stayed in SA or gone back to Ireland. The emotional rollercoaster we had all experienced for the past three and a half months had left us drained, and now having to leave Jade for a few months until she could join us was not what I wanted to do. Logically, I knew we could not go back but had to knuckle down and continue onto the USA. We managed to get a great deal on Lufthansa which would fly us from Johannesburg to Frankfurt where we would have a five-hour layover and then on to Phoenix, Arizona. The flight was booked, and we had a week to get ready. Now I really did not want to go as after all this time waiting it seemed so sudden. We telephoned a few friends and family and some even made trips to Witbank to come and see us and say goodbye. Over the next few days, we prepared getting clothes washed and packed. Jade was also getting ready to leave as she would be staying with Elizabeth in Johannesburg for the few months that she would need to wait for her green card. We knew that after leaving South Africa the weather would get much colder, so we had to keep warm clothes in our hand luggage to change when we landed in Frankfurt.

The day finally arrived, and Brian drove us to the airport. We were met by Terence's other sister Jeanette and my friend, Elizabeth. After checking in our luggage, we still had a few hours to wait, so we all went to a restaurant for potentially our last meal in South Africa. I was trying to be brave as we all chatted and promised to stay in touch, however all I could think was that I was leaving one of my children behind. The only consolation I had was that Jade would be with us either within the year or early the following year.

The dancing night sky
Nature has come to rest
As I look to the stars
Night night sweet dreams
Until we meet again

Leaving a sweltering summer in South Africa, we arrived in Frankfurt in the middle of winter. It was freezing and so before anything else we all headed to the restrooms to change into our winter clothes we had in our carry-on luggage. As we settled into our meal at one of the restaurants Terence checked all our paperwork once again.

I could not help thinking of Jade and wondering how she was doing. We did not have any cell phones as we were going to get new ones in the USA. I so badly wanted to text or call her, but I just had to pray over her and have faith she was doing well. We finally boarded the plane and as I looked out the window, I could see that the aircraft maintenance was spraying the wings with anti-freeze to stop them from freezing. Something I had never seen before.

PART FOUR

THE UNITED STATES OF AMERICA

2004-PRESENT

We had flown nonstop from Frankfurt to Sky Harbor in Phoenix and were more than ready after 17 hours to disembark and stand on solid ground. We had watched movie after movie, eaten the meals that were provided plus snacks, and wandered the isles making acquaintances with some of the other passengers. Upon disembarking, we entered the large area where international passengers from every corner of the globe were lining up waiting for customs.

We looked around finding the line we had to join for persons with green cards immigrating to the USA. I was very nervous not knowing what to expect as we were told that you could even be denied your permanent green cards at your port of entry.

Terence made sure that we all had our envelopes with all our paperwork, x-rays, and passports — everything that needed to be handed in to the immigration officials. The line moved slowly toward the officers standing behind a large brown counter.

Everything seemed to move in slow motion and somehow so quickly all at the same time, and the next thing I knew it was our turn! I was shaking on the inside, this was it, make or break.

After breaking the official seal of the envelope, he started to go through all of our paperwork. He nodded his approval handing back our envelopes and with a smile said "Welcome to America."

I wanted to cry. So much tension over the last few months had suddenly come to an end, as we walked towards the luggage carousel I was in a complete daze.

After retrieving our large suitcases, two golf bags, and the sensitive luggage consisting of fishing gear and a large painting of the Sapekoe tea estates in Tzaneen. The painting was my last reminder of home. It had been with me from South Africa to Ireland back to South Africa and now the United States of America. We walked through the glass doors into the international arrival area to be met by Terence's mom and dad, Douglas and Ernest. They were all smiling and with hugs and kisses welcomed us to the USA. Ernest had a white SUV, and as the men loaded our suitcases, I filled in the news from back home with Terence's mom. We left Sky harbor and joined the traffic on I10 heading for Tucson.

It's amazing to me that no matter where I had lived in the world the sky seemed to be unique to that place, and this was no different. The huge expanse of the Southwestern sky seemed to carry on forever, and the winter sun had just started to set painting the sky with indigo, pink and orange. It was my first American sky, and I'll never forget it! I asked our nephew if I could borrow his phone to text Jade and let her know that we had arrived safely.

The desert sky
Clear at night
I see the stars
Shine o so bright

Even though my heart was happy that, after all these years, we had finally made it to the U.S. it still ached at being separated from Jade, and I prayed that God would take care of her and protect her until she would be able to join us. I sat in the back seat with the painting balancing against my knees. I looked down at the painting, the brightly dressed ladies picking the top leaves of the tea bushes. I closed my eyes and could smell Africa.

Later that evening, Ruth met us at the house that had been rented for us. She was over the moon to have us in the States, especially her brother. The house was an older house and was set in a cul-de-sac. There were five bedrooms and three bathrooms. The living, dining and TV room were spacious and open plan. The backyard was grassed, and there was a large swimming pool nestled in the corner of the garden. Between our immediate family and our nephew's family we had a full functional home from flat wear to bedlinen, we were so blessed.

That night as I laid in bed, I thought of Jade. I was already missing her so much and prayed that we would be reunited soon! I soon fell into a deep sleep not knowing what tomorrow would bring. We had taken a huge step so late in our lives and with only one thousand dollars to our names I hoped that this was the right decision.

After two weeks our official green cards arrived in the mail and we hit the ground running. We applied for our Social Security cards, joined the local library (which was important to me), and Terence got his American driver's license. We had our first meal at Red Robin, and we discovered the enormity of a Walmart Mega Store. I felt like a hamster in one of those wheels going around and around.

Terence and Joffre both struggled to get work. They put in their resumes at numerous businesses, spending hours in the truck that

Ernest and his wife Terri had loaned us driving in some instances for miles. The main concern of the people doing the interviews was that they did not have American resumes or did not study in the USA. How could we have any of the qualifications they required when we had only been in the county a few weeks? They just shrugged telling them it was not their problem. One afternoon, we decided to take a break and walk around the mall. I saw that one of the retail stores were hiring, and I inquired about a job. I was scheduled an interview the very next day and was blessed to be offered the job!

After weeks of waiting for phone calls that were never returned, Joffre bought a shovel and wheelbarrow and started landscaping for a few people in the area where we were living. Terence eventually got a job at a golf and tennis resort raking bunkers and cleaning the bathrooms. We were shocked when he had to go for a drug test, this was yet another new thing we had to get used to in the U.S. Terence worked extremely hard which paid off, he is now a foreman and enjoying the job immensely, wishing he had done this years ago. Joffre was later offered a job training as an electrician with Ernest, where he stayed for two years.

At the same time in South Africa, Jade had started a temporary position at one of the top corporate banks in South Africa with Elizabeth. She enjoyed it immensely and was promoted and given a permanent job in the accounts department within six months. She had never done any accounting before, but she picked it up so quickly that within a year she was the travel accounts payable specialist for the entire bank country wide! She also made a very good friend at the bank named Jen. They bonded immediately with their sense of humor, adventurous spirit and strong faith. Jen was a strong woman of God, and she helped Jade through some tough times. Jen had helped Jade a lot at work and gave her advice for her career as well as in her personal circumstances.

Jade had made another wonderful Christian friend at work, and he invited her to join his bible study once a week and eventually she started to attend this church called Northcliff Union Church. I could not believe it when she told me as that was the same church I used to attend as a little girl in Johannesburg!

We had been in the United States for almost a month, and we really wanted to get a puppy. We started to ask around where we could go to get a rescue puppy and most people suggested the local animal shelter. We checked the days and times they were open, the following week Terence and his parents, Joffre and I headed for the shelter. Terence's parents waited in the car and the three of us went in through the front doors. Once inside, we met a lady at reception, and we explained that we were looking for a puppy. We had to fill out the standard paperwork and once that was done, she took us into caged areas which were filled with every kind of dog from puppies to senior dogs.

There were pure breeds as well as mongrels, each one had those sad eyes that just pierced your heart. Different dogs and puppies were placed together in large, caged areas. The cages were extremely clean, and a faint smell of disinfectant filled the air. There was a sense of hope and expectancy emanating from all the puppies and dogs, and I wished I had a huge farm so that I could take them all home with me.

As Joffre walked past an enclosure of puppies, a black fluffy ball came up to the wire giving him just one small bark, as if to say, "here I am — adopt me!" Joffre put his hand through the fence and patted her head. She was beautiful, but there were so many others we had yet to see. We walked around the area looking and patting all different shapes, sizes, and colors of puppies. We had walked the whole area and when we came back passed the cage with the black puppy. Joffre put out his hand, and she once again bounded to the wire and gave Joffre another bark this time wagging her small tail. Joffre petted her and as she licked his hand, he looked at Terence and me, and we all thought the same thing. This is the one. We realized that Joffre had not chosen her, she had chosen him. With our decision made, the volunteer who had been helping us took us back to reception where we filled out our official puppy adoption forms. We were told that the puppy would have to be spayed and only then could we officially take her home.

We left the shelter feeling excited about the new member of our family. The only thing we had to do now was to come up with a name. After trying out a couple of names we decided to call her Megan, a reminder of our time in Ireland. Joffre chose Diane as her second name, so it was decided Megan Diane Gerber.

Terence's parents spent some quality time with us before they had to leave to go back to South Africa. We were extremely sad to say goodbye, it seemed like the last thread of home had been cut. Sadly, Terence's dad passed away soon after they returned home. Unfortunately, since he had just started a new job it was impossible for him to go for the funeral.

In early March 2004, Terence applied on behalf of Jade to get a green card, he would be her sponsor. We wondered why Jade's application from 1991 could not be used, but according to the immigration office all previous applications were considered null and void, and we had to start again, it just seemed so futile.

In April, Jade had her university graduation. We were so upset that we could not be there for her. Elizabeth and Jen went to support her, and the three of them had a great time!

Our first summer in Tucson was upon us. It was something we were not used to in the least. It was extremely dry and hot. Stepping outside was like stepping into an oven. The dry hot wind was unbearable, we were so grateful for the swimming pool and spent most of the summer swimming well into the evening. Megan did not like the water at all but would love to run around the pool barking at us as we swam.

During the baseball season, Terence, Joffre and I were invited to watch a game at the local stadium. Terence used to play at school and was a huge fan. This was our first live baseball ever. We had seen them on TV, and they always looked like they were full of family fun! We had a great time participating in the singing with everyone else, cheering the team and of course eating hot dogs.

USA USA oh USA
Baseball a favorite pass-time
For all to share
Hot dog hot dog
Get your hot dog
Three strikes and you are out of here
Home run your team has won
USA USA oh USA

We had heard about a six-year visa that a person could apply for if they had a university degree. Jade had a degree in zoology and genetics as a second major. She sent us all the paperwork that was required. We filled out the forms in October 2004 and sent the forms to the Evaluation Service Inc., (International Academic Credential Assessment) in Hopewell Junction, N.Y.

The outcome of the assessment was that Jade would have to study an additional year at an American University to obtain enough credits for a full degree. Even though she had already graduated with a full degree in South Africa, this was not recognized by any employers in the USA.

In November 2004, she applied for a visitor's visa, we were so excited believing she would get it and why not? She called us just after the interview in tears, she was denied. Except when Jade was an exchange student to Argentina in 1997, this was going to be our first Christmas apart.

Jade then decided to join the Athletes in Action team at her church. She and her team were officially trained as counselors, and in December they travelled to Plettenburg bay in the Eastern Cape on a mission trip where they spent time coaching beach volleyball and touch rugby and ministering the word of God.

I could not believe that it was Christmas time already and that we had been in the USA for almost a year. This was my first Christmas in such a huge department store, I had been assigned to the Home Department which I loved. One day, I got to work still saddened by the fact that Jade would not be joining us, everyone in my department was buzzing with excitement as The Christmas Shop was always set up in our area. I was delighted, my favorite time of the year, and I get to help decorate nine trees plus the whole Christmas shop. I worked with a wonderful team of ladies which made it all that more fun! We played Christmas music, had samples of all the edible goodies we were selling, and our manager ran a competition for the best decorated tree. I was thrilled when one of my co-workers and myself won gift cards for the best tree!

Since Terence and I were married, except for the previous Christmas at Brian's house, we always had a live tree for Christmas. Somehow the artificial trees did not seem right. I think because they lacked the gorgeous pine smell. Our first Christmas in the USA was no different. We bought a beautiful Douglas Fir from the local Home Depot which was a lot of fun. We had only seen Christmas tree lots in the movies where people would walk around the lots bundled in winter woollies and snow flurries to capture the mood. Sadly, we had no snow, but we were bundled against the winter chill with brightly colored beanies, jackets and scarves. After loading the tree, we headed for home where we set it up in the TV room and decorated it with blue and silver baubles and tinsel. With the lights ready, we turned off the house lights, and the tree looked perfect as it sparkled and lit up the whole room making it warm and festive. Jade loves Christmas trees and it was always her favorite pastime to choose the perfect tree and decorate it. Jade would love this tree!

Christmas Eve was always held at Ruth's house. Family and friends came from all over to celebrate with us. Michael, Ruth's younger son would always drive down from Phoenix spending the holidays with the family. Ernest, Terri and their children would arrive with their extended family members with gifts which they placed under the Christmas tree in the living room. Ruth's house was a hub of festivities and decorations. She decorated the front garden with beautiful colored Christmas lights thread through the fence and hedges that surrounded the garden. The inside of her house was wonderfully decorated, with tinsel and lights and ornaments galore. The kitchen exuded wonderful and appetizing smells. Her back veranda accommodated three long trestle tables where we gathered to eat. Heaters were placed on either side of the veranda to keep us warm as we dished up and ate an amazing Christmas meal. Once our tummies were full, we went into the house and gathered around the tree to give and receive gifts.

2005

The new year had come and gone so much faster than expected, and it was now suddenly April. We were told that the house we were renting would be needed for the landlord's son. We had two months to find a new place. As anyone knows finding a new home is not that easy, but we had started looking for a new home. Terence's mom was out visiting for another six months, this time on her own, so she spent a lot more time with us. On our days off, Terence, Joffre, Terence's mom and I drove around Tucson looking at apartments, townhouses and houses. Since we could only afford two secondhand cars which Joffre and Terence drove. I was very nervous to drive in the U.S., so we had to find a home near a bus stop so that I could use the public transport to get to work. We would also ideally like a small garden for Megan. After nearly a month of searching, and lots of prayer, one of my co-workers mentioned that there was a townhouse for sale in her sister's home association complex. We decided to take a look at the house, and it was perfect! During this time that we were waiting for the final paperwork etc., we lived in an RV borrowed from Ernest and Terri outside Ruth's house. It was interesting to say the least. Joffre, Megan and Terence's mom lived inside the house with Ruth, while Terence and I were in the RV.

With the uncertainty of how long her green card would take to be issued and now not sure how long she would be in SA, Jade needed a more permanent living situation. In March 2005, she moved out of Elizabeth's house and moved in with Terence's sister Jeanette who was also in Johannesburg. She was still working at the bank and was having a highly successful career there.

In May 2005, we received a letter stating that Jade's petition for a green card, that was submitted by Terence in 2004, had been in theory approved and sent to the National Visa Centre for further processing. Now we knew it would not take long for her green card. In August 2005, we were contacted once again by the National Visa Center and were told that they were only processing visa applications from the year 1996. This meant that it would take a further nine years before Jade's would come up for review.

The news was once again devastating, her green card would take years, and this was not what we were led to believe? What was going on? Had they made a mistake? We eventually consoled ourselves with the fact that at least she would be home for holidays, we would make it more than once a year. I did not like our situation; I did not like my job, and I certainly did not like the USA. I wanted to go back to Ireland so badly.

In the beginning of 2005, Jade had also started acting out of character, she started drinking and clubbing a lot. It was not all the time, but when she went out it was an all-nighter with too many vodka-redbulls. (I guess this was her way of dealing with our separation.) She was very emotional all the time, she suddenly started to notice that her hair was falling out in clumps and that she was having a lot of back and joint pain. This continued for about six months, and in August she made an appointment to see a doctor to find out what was going on. He was very sympathetic and after hearing all her symptoms he started to ask about her personal life and if she was happy etc. All of a sudden, she burst into tears and told him the story of our separation. He did a few tests and told her that she was suffering from clinical depression and would have to go on medication. She could not understand and told him she did not feel depressed and why would she need pills. He told her that she was suppressing her feelings and not allowing them to surface, but that the symptoms in the rest of her body were signs of depression manifesting itself. She did not want to take the meds and so asked if there was an alternative. The doctor booked her off work for ten days and told her she had to take a vacation.

About that time, Ruth was heading to the SA for a visit. Terence's brother and sisters and mom very kindly took Jade on a vacation to Moloth park, a beautiful park where Jeanette had a house. It is a group of privately-owned houses which boarder on the Kruger National Park. She had an amazing time, and it was good to get out of the city. However, after a week of being back at work her symptoms starting to return and she was put on eighteen months of anti-depressants.

During this time, Jade and Jeanette got very close and spent a lot of time together. Jeanette was taking care of her and would take her out on runs and social events at her running club. She was always Jade's plus one to any of Jade's bank's social events. She also made sure that Jade was eating healthy and keeping busy with friends and activities on the weekends from drama classes to scuba-diving.

That October, Jade was thinking of coming to visit us again and the doctor also gave her a letter stating that she needed to see her family and the separation was the cause of her clinical depression. However, she decided to stay in Johannesburg and instead she joined her Athletes in Action teammates and headed down to Plettenburg Bay for two weeks in December. She said that the potential rejection was too much and that she would try again, if she still did not have her green card by December 2006.

One day on my lunch break, I was walking through the mall looking for a birthday gift for Terence. I was walking past the bookstore when I saw a book by Pastor Joel Osteen called *Your Best Life Now*. It was displayed in the window under "New Releases". I decided to go in and have a look. I read the back of the book and thought it would make the perfect gift for Terence.

I mentioned the book to Jade, and she found it as her local Christian bookstore. She also found him on TV in South Africa and loved his message of hope. Jade and her Aunt Janette would regularly watch his program. Reading Pastor Joel's book and watching his messages really helped her. She started to be more and more encouraged and eventually, she was told that she could stop her anti-depressants six months earlier than planned! It certainly was the right word at the right time for her.

We continued to call every day, it was the only way we were able to stay in touch because Jade did not have a land line. We had to call her on her cell phone, we also e-mailed her constantly. Her safety was another huge concern, and we suggested various jobs that would take her out of the country, none of them up to this point worked out. I had been reading the story about Joshua in my quiet time. When I read chapter two about Rahab helping the two spies, I had an idea. If Rahab, all those hundreds of years ago, had a scarlet rope hanging from her window having faith that God was working in her situation, then what was stopping me from hanging a scarlet ribbon from our home. The following day I called Jade and we decided that she would hang a scarlet ribbon from her bedroom window, and we would hang one at our front door. A declaration that we had faith that God was working in our situation. To this day a rather faded ribbon still hangs at our front door.

A land so big
Come let us go
Up to the top
Let us watch
Let us see
As the desert speaks

One day, Jade got home from work to find police cars in front of the house. The house where she was staying had been broken into. She walked inside and there was stuff everywhere! It looked like a movie scene, clothes strewn all over the floors of the bedrooms, draws open and empty, and the police were there taking finger-prints. After she called to tell us this, we were even more worried. We shudder to think what would have happened if she had been home when they had broken into the house. We thank God that she was not there when this happened. I know that she did not sleep that night at all.

One evening that December, it was bitterly cold. I was talking to Jade on the phone, she was now in Plettenburg Bay with her Athletes in Action team. Her team was tremendously supportive and once again she had an amazing time. She is a great counselor and has a light that others are just drawn to, and even though she was struggling she was still helping others. It is so true what the Word of God says in Proverbs 11, that as you refresh others you yourself will be refreshed. Later that same evening, Terence was taking out the trash when he heard a faint little mew, he looked up and sitting on the sidewalk outside our house was a grey tabby cat. She was just sitting there looking at the house. Terence approached her and she ran into the neighbor's garden. As he climbed into bed Terence told me what had happened, but we did not think any more of it. The next evening Terence was taking out the trash and there, sitting on the sidewalk staring at the house was the little cat. We decided to put out a bowl of water and food and a cardboard box with a warm blanket. She appeared to be an adult cat, but she was very cold and skinny, so it was hard to tell just how young or old she really was. For the next two weeks, we continued to feed her and were delighted that she was using the box to stay warm. During this time, we tried to find out who owned her. We contacted everyone we could think of but nothing. One night, we decided to see if she would come inside. We opened our backdoor and the little grey tabby trotted into the house. She was right at home and fit into our family as if she had always been there. She was lovely and a real little lady. We called her Miss Kitty, and her and Megan became fast friends.

This year Jade was not able to get the week of Christmas off instead she only got a few days around Christmas day. Jeanette had already made plans to join Brian at his house. Jade was so friendly and wanted to be friends with everyone and so after a few short weeks she had become friends with all her neighbors on Jeanette's street. She became particularly close to a family that lived opposite Janette. Dorothy and Denzil had lived there for years and had two children Lee and Carol. Jade somehow fit in with their family seamlessly and was almost like an older sister to the children and a good friend of Dorothy. She would look after their home and pets when they went on vacation, and when Janette was not home, she would spend most of her time with them. This year she spent Christmas with them.

I was so grateful that God had given her a family that she could celebrate and spend Christmas with. She would not be alone.

2006

All I can say is that a family's prayers are always answered. Jade came away from that ministry happy and full of a renewed purpose to follow God and encourage others.

When Jade went back to work in 2006, she started a small bible study that would meet every morning in one of the conference rooms. It was a small group of co-workers from her department. They would take 30 minutes to read some scripture Jade had prepared and then discuss and encourage each other. Jade also typed up notes of the scripture and handed it out to those who were there as a summary of their time together. Word got around about what she was doing and eventually there were those that could not attend that would ask for the notes for personal devotional time. It got to the point that she was handing out notes from the lunch ladies in the cafeteria to one of the executives on the top floor of the company who even had his secretary start a special binder just for Jade's daily devotional notes.

God was really working in and through her. And I was so proud of what she was doing.

I wish many things
Many things for you
But most of all
Let love shine all around the world

In October 2006, on her fourth visit to the U.S Consulate to apply for a Visitor's visa for Christmas, a very kind consular officer who was doing Jade's interview asked if anyone had told her or us for that matter, what the real reason was behind all her visa denials. Jade told her no. The kind lady then proceeded to tell her that if she had a green card pending, she would never be granted a visitor's visa. It took four visits for someone to tell her this? We could have been saved a lot of heartache and disappointment if we had known this from the beginning.

This particular consular officer was horrified that number one Jade had been separated from her family by U.S. Immigration, secondly that no-one had bothered to tell her how a pending green card would affect her visiting status. During the same time (2004-2006), we were trying everything we knew from our side of the globe. We had no money for lawyer's fees to take on this long and tedious fight, but were advised that no matter what we did it would not change the U.S. Immigration laws. We felt that at least we could try and maybe get someone to help us.

We then wrote to the congress representative, two of our senators and the governor. The two senators required us to fill out confidentiality forms which we returned. Only one senator replied suggesting that we enter Jade's name in the State Diversity Lottery Program. Once again, we filled out the required paperwork. Because we did not have a computer and it needed urgent attention as we only had a few days to do it, we asked a friend to forward all the forms plus a photo to the given website. We felt quite positive that this might work. A few days later we discovered that he had not done it and the date had lapsed. I was so annoyed, what was wrong with people, why was it such a trivial thing for them. I was getting more and more disgusted with the whole immigration system.

We had recently found a local church, and the pastor had heard about our dilemma with Jade's immigration. He asked us to come into his office the following week for an informal meeting, mentioning he had a friend in Washington D.C. who he was sure could help us. I was thrilled but Terence said not to get our hopes up, but I so desperately wanted it to work. The following week we arrived for our meeting at the church. Every time I relayed our story I got a lump in my throat; this was getting harder and harder and I wanted someone to wave a "magic wand" and rectify the mess. He said that he would speak to his friend on our behalf. He was so upbeat and positive giving us much needed hope. We decided not to tell Jade until we had more definite news. Each week we attended church, but the pastor did not mention his friend, and we did not ask we figured it would take at least a month or two before we heard anything. About four weeks later we were sitting in church when it was announced from the stage that the pastor wanted to say a few words. In a strained tearful voice, he told the congregation that he was handing in his resignation with immediate effect. Sadly, and extremely selfishly, I thought, *what about us, what about your friend in D.C., where does this leave us?* It was all about us, all about ME in those few minutes. We had a chance to speak to the pastor and his wife before they drove away. As much as I wanted to, I did not bring up the subject of his friend helping us. I felt horribly guilty at my previous thoughts; needless to say, my spirit spiraled to an all-time low. We then heard that the pastor had started a new church on the other side of town, we were asked by some of the church folk who followed him if we would care to join them. Terence, Joffre, and I were keen to join as we enjoyed his preaching and his upbeat and positive attitude. The subject of his friend in D.C. was never mentioned by him again.

A petition was then draw up and signed by members of the church and with our permission was to be sent to the White House. Having the church members behind us we felt we had a chance of getting someone's attention. The list and a letter were duly sent to the White House, we waited in anticipation. The reply came a few weeks later; there was nothing they could do to help. A return letter from the President's office stated that the issuance of visas was controlled by the USCIS (U.S Citizenship and Immigration Services) and therefore, the State Department could not assist. Shortly after this the pastor resigned and the church closed its doors.

Our hopes were raised when a new congress representative was elected to our area in 2006. By now we knew the problem with her visitation rights were due to the pending green card.

2007

In the early part 2007, Terence, Joffre and myself went to the congress offices to see if they could help us in any way. We spoke to a very pleasant young man who after about 15 minutes admitted that Terence knew more than he did about the immigration system. We duly filled out the forms he gave us, telling us that they would be in touch. The following day a person from the congress office called telling us there was nothing they could do. Quite a number of people suggested that we bring Jade over the border, their reasoning was that so many illegal people come across with no consequence that why shouldn't she. Even though it sounded good, 'just bring her across' we knew that there were more negative than positive factors, but the law is the law and if she was to come to the U.S. we would do it legally, no matter how long it took. We were now living in the USA and had to abide by the laws of the country. Many people we had spoken to over the years were horrified, they had no idea what it entailed to immigrate.

A few months into 2007, we started planning a family reunion. At the same time in South Africa Jade was planning to move to England. We were going to wait for her to get her visa and get settled in England, and we were going to meet up with her there.

Jen took Jade to the company where she would be submitting her application for a two-year working holiday visa. They sat in the car and Jen prayed over Jade's paperwork. They knew that if God was with them nothing could stop it.

When she applied for a two-year working visa for the United Kingdom, she was rejected purely due to the fact that the USA had rejected her numerous times when she applied for visitors' visas to come and see us. She was told that if the USA was not letting her into their country then neither were they. In the end, she wrote a letter to the British Consular explaining that she had been approved for a green card and was waiting for her paperwork to be processed. She had been rejected for visits to the USA but accepted for immigration. Under advisement, she handed in her appeal to the British Consulate. Not expecting any answer soon Jade left the outcome to God and moved on with life and so did we. We now had to start looking for a new place to meet up. With living expenses and a mortgage, we had very little money so decided a holiday in Mexico would be ideal.

Terence, Joffre and I would drive to a place we selected to holiday, this would leave only one air ticket to purchase, Jade's. The accommodation would, we were sure, be more in our price range. When Jade went to book her ticket in Johannesburg, she discovered that she had a short layover in Los Angeles. Due to her pending green card she was not allowed to disembark in L.A. or on any American soil for any amount of time. This situation was really becoming bizarre and increasingly annoying. We spoke about flying back to South Africa, but it was far too expensive, so we decided to go back to the Rep. of Ireland for two weeks. Joffre paid for half the holiday and the balance we put onto our "emergency credit card", as this had become an emergency situation.

After arranging all the tickets and bookings to Ireland, Jade suddenly got an e-mail in the beginning of August to say that she had now been granted her two-year working holiday visa for England. She would be moving to London in January 2008.

About two weeks before we left for Ireland, Megan, our dog sadly and suddenly passed away. We were devastated. She was such an amazing dog with such a lovely nature and delightful personality. We buried her in our back garden. Later that day, I texted Jade to tell her our sad news. Miss Kitty and Megan had become good friends and for the next few days Miss Kitty wandered the house looking for Megan trying to figure out where her friend had gone. Now more than ever we felt like we needed a holiday. Ruth would take care of Miss Kitty while we were in Ireland.

Late August of 2007 we met up for the first time in three and a half years at the Dublin airport.

We rented a bungalow on the beautiful Beara Peninsular. We found a dead, yet beautiful branch in the garden which we decorated, placing it in the lounge to represent a Christmas tree. We filled one of the lounge windows with colorful balloons representing our birthdays. We had a magical holiday catching up on lost time as well as birthdays and Christmases. We set two days aside for these two celebrations exchanging small gifts, and eating scrumptious treats and cupcakes as birthday cakes.

We did a lot of sightseeing leaving early most mornings and coming home late at night. We took Jade to places we visited while living in Ireland, wanting to share as much as we could. We ate fish and chips on the rocks overlooking the harbor in Dingle, climbed the stairs in Blarney Castle, kissing the stone, played golf in Glengarriff and Castlegregory and Frisbee on the beach at Allihies. On one of the days we caught a rickety old cable car from the mainland to the Dunsery Island, swaying from side to side in freezing winds. We felt like sardines in a rusty old tin. We had three days left in the last part of our holiday together. We left Allihies and made the long drive to Ballaghaderreen. We had arranged to stay with family friends from the church we had attended. It was such a delight to see familiar faces and hear the beautiful lilt of their Irish accents. The house was warm and welcoming.

Over the next two days, we walked through the town popping into various shops to say 'hello' to the owners who we got to know so well when we lived there, a cup of tea and cake would always be offered. The supermarket where we worked had moved to the next street, a new building with all modern fixtures, but the warm welcoming smiles of our old colleges as well as the owner and his family had not changed. Later, we went to the local pub for a light lunch.

The two weeks had come to an end, far too soon. We said incredibly sad goodbyes, promising each other we would not cry. Jade flew back to the South Africa via London. Terence, Joffre and I spent a night in Swords; we flew out the next day.

Once we were back in the United States and settled once again, we continued to check the computer for Jade's status, willing her date to miraculously come up, but there were still years to go.

At this time, Joffre's job with his cousin Ernest ended due to the recession. He applied at the golf and tennis resort where Terence worked. His application was accepted, and he started at the end of September 2007.

This was a real blessing as both Terence and Joffre got to spend all of their time outdoors in nature. Being both born and raised on farms, this really suited them as they were constantly surrounded by the wild, and they would often come home telling me about all the wonderful creatures they had seen from ground squirrels to bobcats!

The eagle has landed
Coyotes running wild
The cool of the morning
And the wet dew around
Another day in the desert sun

2008

Suddenly it was January 2008, and Jade had left South Africa for London. We were so relieved that she had finally made it out of Johannesburg and away from all the danger. It was a difficult move for her doing everything on her own, but she was resilient and independent. We would have loved to go over to the England to help her settle in, but we still did not have any extra money.

Jade had found a comfortable family home in the Southwest of London where she was renting a room. The house was across the street from the local tennis club which she had joined. Jade also met a wonderful friend at the club called Patrick. He was so kind and generous, and they became very good friends. He helped her in so many ways!

In early 2008, very unexpectantly, Terence won two thousand dollars on the lottery. This meant I was able to go to London to help Jade settle into her new way of life, an answer to prayer. In early April, Terence and Joffre drove me up to Sky Harbor in Phoenix, where for the first time I had to fly alone, I was petrified! With much prayer all went well. Most of my luggage was made up of linens and clothing we had bought for her in the United States. On a cold spring morning, I landed at Heathrow where I was met by Jade cradling a large, beautiful spring bouquet of yellow lilies and purple irises.

She had started working at a commodities firm on Oxford Street, so she did not have much time off. The time we were able to spend together (weekends and some days off) was real quality time. We went to the theatre, visited lovely gardens, and took in all the usual tourist sites. The weather was freezing, but that did not spoil our fun. At night we would lie in bed (we shared a double bed) talking into the wee hours. Once again, time had flown by, and I was packing to go back to the U.S. Jade saw me off at Heathrow. Tears flowed as the plane taxed off.

Trying to be brave was becoming more and more difficult.

I was still having quite a few 'pity parties' some days feeling more despondent than others. I kept thinking to myself *"was this the way it was always going to be from now on? Just two week visits every three to four years? Were we ever going to be able to be together as a family again?"* Some days it just seemed easier to pack up and give up on the whole American thing and find another country that would be willing to at least let a family be together.

Working in the department store and constantly dealing with the public did not make it any easier. On many occasions mothers would come in to buy items for their children that had moved away from home for various reasons. They would tell me how they missed their child/children; how they wished they could visit them more, how they wished they lived closer. I would ask where they lived only to be told that it was either an hour way or a short plane trip away. Really? Were these people being serious? At least they could still see their children whenever they wanted. Some of them had literally just moved down the road! I started to resent these women who had no idea how lucky they were. I wanted so badly for my daughter to just be in the same country as me. I would try hard not to show my irritation.

It was especially difficult for me seeing mothers and daughters out shopping and enjoying each other's company. One morning at work, I was doing stock when a lady walked up to get some help.

As the store was particularly quiet that day, we started chatting. After being asked I ended up telling her the saga of the green card and how Jade could not visit. She let me continue my whining and moaning, as I would to anyone who would listen to my story, without saying a word.

She was so gracious and said she could understand my feelings and knew how hard it was not to have a daughter around. I thought to myself — her daughter was probably just a plane or car ride away like all the others I had spoken to over the years. I then asked her more about her daughter and she started to cry. She said she had died in an accident two months earlier at the age of sixteen. I felt so embarrassed and ashamed I wanted to crawl in a hole. What a wakeup call. I could have lost my daughter like she did; my daughter was at least still alive. I could at least speak to her every day, and I would get to see her again — even if it was in a few years' time. Suddenly the years did not seem to matter, all that mattered was that we would be able to see each other again. I then decided that I needed to change my attitude in a big way. It would take some time, but it had to be done.

One morning while eating my breakfast before work I was feeling a little low. I started flicking through the television channels and stopped at "Enjoying Everyday Life" with Joyce Meyer. I felt quite inspired as she was teaching on how our attitude can affect your daily life — wow! That was just what I needed to hear. It was a great message, and so the following day I found myself eating my breakfast and watching her program once again. Since my hours were different every day and sometimes my schedule was unpredictable, I decided to make this time my personal bible study. I would take notes, read the scriptures, making an effort to put the messages into practice. I was finding my situation becoming a lot easier, my attitude was less negative, and I was actually having more fun. I would sometimes get Terence and Joffre to watch with me. I have a copy of her book *Never Give Up* next to my computer, always a gentle reminder. I found her teaching to be practical and instead of feeling sorry for myself and my situation I decided that it was me that perhaps needed to change.

Instead of being a victim of my situation, I needed to give it to God.

A few months later, I was blessed to meet Joyce at a book signing at our local Barnes and Noble. Unfortunately, there were so many people that we did not have time to talk; I wish I could have told her the impact she had made on my life. I did shake her hand, and we knowingly shared a smile.

On the other side of the Atlantic, Jade was settling into the London lifestyle. She had found an amazing church in central London, and she was a part of the Events and Guest Relations team. She was volunteering and serving with a wonderful group of ladies the same age. Jade was so happy to be a part of this church, and she grew in her relationship with God in leaps and bounds. She spent every spare minute she had volunteering and even using her vacation time off from her day job to serve at large events and conferences. The church as well as her team really changed her life. During the early Sunday mornings and when some special events ran late into the night, Patrick would pick up Jade and some of the ladies from her team who lived in her area and give them lifts home. He was a real blessing to them especially in the Winter. I knew that he was only a phone call away and would help Jade wherever and whenever he could. London would not have been the same without him.

Jade had also befriended a wonderful family in the church who lived just outside of London. She visited them at their home a couple of times, and one Christmas she spent with them, they spoiled her with surprise gifts underneath their Christmas tree. They treated her just like another member of the family and made her feel right at home! They also had lots of pets, and it was lovely for Jade to enjoy walking their dogs and fussing the cats.

It was so nice for me to know that there were people around her that were taking care of her and treating her like family, especially since she could not be with her own. No words could ever express my gratitude for these special people.

If you want to know some simple things
Love what you have and never give in
Walk with pride and never compromise
Trust in God
God's always by your side

2009

In October of 2009, Terence and Joffre decided to become citizens. I was hesitant and still feeling unsettled in the USA, so I decided to do my citizenship when Jade did. No matter how long it took I would remain a green card holder.

We had been in the country over five years now and were eligible. In doing this, it would up Jade's status considerably.

We spoke to our immigration lawyer and the naturalization process was started. The first step would be a verbal exam, and if you passed that the second step would be to be sworn in as citizens. For the first step we were given a book that contained one hundred possible questions and answers about the country, its government and history. From these one hundred a possible ten could be asked by the examiner on the date of the naturalization exam. It was October 2009, when we started the process and the earliest date for the test was for 15th January 2010 for them to do the exam. I spent many hours asking questions from the book they received which ended up been informative as well as great fun, we learned a lot about the country. They had three months to learn everything in the book about the country, and what most people would take for granted. Some of the Americans that we spoke to would sometimes joke and say we knew more about their country than what they did.

2010

On the 10th of January 2010, Terence and Joffre went to do the exam. All went well and a date for step two, them to be sworn in as American Citizens, was set. This would take place on the 25th of January 2010. On the day of the swear-in, we joined a large group of people at the courthouse building. Everyone was jovial, families posing for photos, others recording the day on video. The great room was filled with nationalities from all over the world. Terence and Joffre were the only two South Africans. I proudly clicked my little Kodak instamatic. Sadly, something went wrong with the music and video that was supposed to play the national anthem as well as an address by President Obama, but even with this slight glitch it was a memorable day. We celebrated with a lovely lunch and later had dinner with Ruth.

USA
Red White and Blue
The bold and brave
The land of the free
This is the USA

Now that Terence was a citizen, Jade's date went up by five years, according to the computer her date was due, and we could get her paperwork moving.

By the end of the year Jade could be home!

During all the years, I felt Joffre was our "rock". One of the things he made sure of is that his Dad would not become a "couch potato". Joffre had his Dad out playing golf in all weather.

If we had the same days off Joffre would suggest a place of interest to visit or a place to go and eat. A few times we went to play golf at other golf courses around the area where we lived. Every year he would buy tickets for the Accenture Match Play at Dove Mountain, it was always a fun time being out on the course, and it was like another world away from the everyday routine. It has become a yearly event for us. Joffre was always positive when speaking to Jade on the phone never once a negative word even though he was feeling the separation from her as much as Terence and I.

By the 4th of March 2010, we were told that Jade would be home in December 2010, still no definite date. We prayed that it would be before Joffre's birthday on the 20th of December and Christmas. We only have a two-bedroom town-house. Joffre suggested we make the Arizona Room a bedroom for Jade and not to partition it off as we wanted to. Joffre re-vamped the bathroom that they would be sharing. Terence and Joffre also did a lot of work to make the Arizona room more of a bedroom. I think our rescue cat, Miss Kitty, could also feel the excitement as it began to mount.

Jade left London and flew back to South Africa, like us, she had to emigrate from her country of birth. She had to go through much the same process as we had to. Most of the paperwork was done in the United States. Jade was offered her old job back in Johannesburg while she was still in London and so during the four months that she waited in South Africa she was able to pass the time by working, as none of us knew how long this process was actually going to take. She was also living with Jeanette again; however Jeanette was coming to the USA for five weeks on vacation.

I was a little concerned as she would be alone in this big house (that had previously been broken into). The next day, Jade called me and told me that Dorothy and Denzil invited her to stay in their home for the five weeks. She joined them for church every Sunday for the few months that she was in South Africa. Once again, God had answered my prayers and provided her safety and a home.

On the 14th of November 2010, Jade was contacted advising her that her interview date at the American Consulate was scheduled for the 14th of December. Nerves set in for her as well as for us, we knew that she could still be denied.

Her interview at the consulate went very well; everyone was friendly and helpful. We were so grateful she did not have all the problems we had. For the first time in many visits, Jade left the consulate smiling and happy. The consular officer said that the visa would be ready in three days; however there was a public holiday on the Thursday which meant it would be ready on the following Monday. This would mean that she would land the day after Joffre's birthday on the 21st of December. She asked if it was at all possible that the visa would be ready sooner.

They then asked her if she was able to come in and collect the visa, when she said that she was able to they said they would have the visa ready within twenty-four hours! She was so excited she called us all immediately, and then went and bought champagne and chocolates for everyone in the office! Most of her co-workers had known her since she was young and even referred to her as the baby in the office, so they were thrilled to hear she would finally be with her family as they had been on this journey with her too. The next day she went to go and collect her visa and was warned that even though she had the visa she could still be deported by customs officials at her port of entry. That evening when she got home, she booked her flight! She was able to get one of the last seats on a direct flight to Atlanta on Saturday evening. This meant that she would arrive in Phoenix on Sunday morning which was the 19th of December 2010, a day before Joffre's birthday and in time for Christmas, an answer to prayer!

The day before she left Dorothy, Denzil, Lee, and Carol had organized a farewell braai and had invited friends and family to come and say farewell to Jade. It was the perfect day filled with laughter, swimming, and time spent with those who matter most.

The morning of December 19th dawned crisp and clear. Ruth was driving us to airport, Sky Harbor in Phoenix. Michael and his girlfriend would meet us there. It was such a momentous occasion for us all, and he wanted to treat us all to lunch once Jade had arrived. We had bought a bunch of pink Inca Lilies, some brightly colored balloons and small American flags to welcome Jade to the United States and home. Before we left the house, we did a last-minute check to make sure everything was ready. Joffre had bought her a basket full of welcoming gifts which we placed on her bed. As I turned to leave the room I smiled, my heart was overjoyed! The trip to the airport seemed to go on forever even though it was only an hour and a half drive. About halfway, we all became quiet, each one in their own thoughts. The long haul was coming to an end; it was hard to get my head around where we were and what the four of us had been through. As I gazed out of the car window, I looked up and said a quiet prayer of thanks to our Heavenly Father for caring us through the past seven years. This was going to be one of the longest waits of my life. Terence could not sit still. He was wandering around checking his watch every five minutes. The rest of us got comfortable and waited. Then Jade's flight was announced, my heart skipped a beat, this was it. Soon passengers from her flight started to file into arrivals. Minutes before we were united one of the balloons, a big silver star with a red ribbon somehow disentangled itself from the rest. It floated high into the terminal building shimmering as it caught the sunlight.

As I watched the balloon float up into the air, the red ribbon reminded me of faith and no matter what, God is faithful. Our daughter and sister were in our arms, home at last.

USA, Ireland, South Africa
I never thought I would say these words
But now I say it because it is true
These three countries
I am sharing them with you.

CPSIA information can be obtained
at www.ICGtesting.com
Printed in the USA
FSHW020957191021
85462FS